WHERE WATERS RUN
BEAVERS

NorthWord
WILDLIFE SERIES

Photography © 1997: Doug Locke/Dembinsky Photo Associates, Front cover;
Joe McDonald/Bruce Coleman, Inc., 1; Art Wolfe, 4-5; Len Rue, Jr., 6, 69, 76-77, 119,
120-121; Robert McCaw, 8-9, 13, 39, 40, 42-43, 62-63, 66, 82, 91, 92-93, 113, 129, 141;
Erwin & Peggy Bauer/Bruce Coleman, Inc., 10, Back cover; Des & Jen Bartlett/Bruce
Coleman, Inc., 14-15, 103; Sharon & Ray Bailey/F-Stock, Inc., 16-17, 34-35; Tom & Pat
Leeson, 19, 22, 26, 50, 53, 59, 64, 73, 80-81, 86, 89, 104-105, 109, 134-135, 137, 142; Jim
Brandenburg/Minden Pictures, 21, 31, 48-49, 61; Leonard Lee Rue III/Bruce Coleman,
Inc., 25, 96, 125; Paul Dalzell/F-Stock, Inc., 28-29; Dominique Braud/Dembinsky Photo
Associates, 32, 56-57; Gary Schultz/The Wildlife Collection, 36, 126; Michael
Francis/The Wildlife Collection, 44, 85; Gary R. Zahm/Bruce Coleman, Inc., 46;
Larry Thorngren/F-Stock, Inc., 55; Jonathan T. Wright/Bruce Coleman, Inc., 70;
Mark Raycroft, 74; Leonard Lee Rue III, 79, 95, 114, 122-123, 138; Norman Owen
Tomalin/Bruce Coleman, Inc., 98-99; Wayne Lankinen/Bruce Coleman, Inc., 100, 130;
Wolfgang Bayer/Bruce Coleman, Inc., 106; Larry Mishkar/F-Stock, Inc., 110;
Scott Nielsen/Bruce Coleman, Inc., 116; Robert Lankinen/The Wildlife Collection,
132-133.

CREATIVE
PUBLISHING
international

NorthWord Press, Inc.
5900 Green Oak Drive
Minnetonka, MN 55343
1-800-328-3895

Book design by Amy J. Quamme

Library of Congress Cataloging-in-Publication Data

Strong, Paul I. V.
        Beavers : where waters run / by Paul Strong.
            p.   cm.—(NorthWord wildlife series)
        Includes bibliographical references.
        ISBN 1-55971-580-4 (sc)
        1. American beaver.   I. Title.   II. Series.
    QL737.R632S78   1997
    599.37—dc21   96-46824

Printed in Singapore

WHERE WATERS RUN
BEAVERS

by Paul Strong

NORTHWORD®
NORTHWORD PRESS
Minnetonka, Minnesota

Dedication

To my daughter, Kalmia Elizabeth Strong, whose sense of wonder of Nature has more than once revitalized my own.

Acknowledgments

As with any undertaking of this magnitude, many people contribute in various ways. I would never have studied beavers or have become a wildlife biologist without John Bissonette who took a risk and offered me a graduate assistantship and who supported me through two and a half years of mistakes and successes.

During my studies of beavers in Big Bend National Park, Texas, this Yankee was taken in by a wonderful community of Park employees and their families who kept me alive both physically and spiritually. My friends in Boquillas, Mexico did the same.

I thank Tom Klein for having the confidence in me to write this book and Barbara Harold, my editor, who exercised just the right combination of patience and pressure to keep me going.

Beavers have been studied for over a century by a wide array of biologists, wildlife managers, and nature observers. Their hours of dedicated observations and experiments in all kinds of harsh conditions were significant contributions to my own limited understanding of these fascinating creatures.

My parents, Charles and Mary Strong, deserve my endless gratitude for teaching me important lessons about life and for offering me opportunities to have the interest, ability, and perseverance to write this and other books.

Donna, your loving support is deeply appreciated.

North America's largest rodent, the beaver is a source
of fascination for nature lovers everywhere.

Preface

That familiar smell jarred something in the deep recesses of my memory and the fly line I had been plying back and forth fell unceremoniously into waist-deep water, no longer a threat to the brook trout in this pool of the Marengo River. A puff of breeze brought the smell again, this time more sharply, and I turned to the wind to seek its source.

There, along the river bank, was an almost unnoticeable mound of freshly scratched mud. Leaving all thoughts of fishing aside for the moment, I waded to shore. Laying down my fly rod, I got down on hands and knees, put my nose to the ground, and inhaled deeply.

The sweet, musky aroma awoke dormant brain cells which began to replay a multitude of events starting in my twenty-first year. Although beavers were not strangers to me before then, it was only as I started to study them intensively that I really became of aware of them. In that crouched posture on the bank of a small northern Wisconsin River, I remembered the specific details of certain days from the past seventeen years, what I was wearing, precisely where I was, who was with me, and what was said.

The locations varied from Canada to Mexico, from remote

beaver ponds in the Quetico Provincial Park to logging roads in northern Maine to the Rio Grande in southwestern Texas. In each place, I had a close encounter with beavers which lodged itself into my memory.

Funny how a smell can bring back such a wealth of past events. Most of us can recall the minute details of our mother's kitchen just from the smell of a freshly baked pie or a favorite meal. The smell of saltwater reminds me of a happy childhood. And for better or worse, the excretions from a beaver's scent glands link me to a period in my life when I had beavers on my mind.

Like smells, the written word and photographs can immediately transport a person to a favorite place and time. In this book, I hope you will come to understand one of nature's truly remarkable animals, the beaver, an adaptable creature if there ever was one. More importantly, I hope the combination of words and photos will transport you to a place or places—a trout stream, a wilderness lake, a creek running through your property, or a slow-moving river—where beavers helped define an unforgettable moment.

9

Beavers are more at home in the water than on land.

Cousin to mice and squirrels, the beaver shares many
of their rodent characteristics.

Meet the Beaver

Like many people who spend a lot of time on rivers and lakes, I thought I knew a lot about beavers. After all, what was there to know? They build dams, construct lodges in which to spend the winter, and cut down trees to feed on the bark. Whenever they saw me in my canoe, they slapped their tails on the water to warn all of the other beavers nearby. Little did I know as a youngster growing up on a lake in central Maine that my path in life would cause me to learn far more about beavers than I ever thought imaginable and that I would learn many of these things in a place far more famous for rattlesnakes and cactus than for northern lights and moose.

I moved from Maine to north-central Oklahoma in search of a Master's degree in wildlife ecology figuring that I would conduct a field research study on a species typical of the Great Plains such as jackrabbits or prairie dogs. Instead, I wound up spending a year in Big Bend National Park, Texas, studying beavers that inhabited the Rio Grande on the Mexican border. Until that time, I wouldn't have guessed that beavers could be found south of the Mason-Dixon line, much less on a slow-moving, silt-laden river winding its way through the heart of the Chihuahuan Desert.

Since that time, I have had beavers on my mind as I have

lived and traveled through Maine and the Great Lakes states. And while I now think I know something about these creatures, I also realize that this intensively studied animal, by scientist, fur trapper, and nature observer alike, remains an alluring and mysterious work of Nature.

The Rat's Cousin

The beaver is a rodent, which means it is closely related to rats, mice, and squirrels. Rodents in general are not held in high esteem. We trap and poison them to keep them away from our stores of food. They are carriers of diseases like the virus that caused the bubonic plague across Europe in the Middle Ages and the more recently discovered Hanta virus. They damage our homes, gnawing at wood and sometimes chewing through electrical wiring. Rodents make us think of small and furtive creatures that scurry across our floors in the night and keep us awake as they run across the ceiling or in the walls.

Although most rodents are small, they found an unfilled niche in some parts of the world which allowed a few species to evolve large body sizes and adapt to an aquatic way of life. The beaver is the second largest species of rodent in the world today exceeded only by the South American capybara, or water hog as it is known locally.

Beavers are truly enormous when viewed in context of their far more familiar and smaller cousin the mouse. While a mouse living comfortably in your attic may attain a weight of an ounce or two, an adult Canadian beaver may weigh as much as ninety pounds. Weights of beavers vary greatly across their North American range with smaller beavers living in the extreme southern areas.

Some of the largest beavers ever recorded were caught in Wisconsin, which is near the center of the beaver's range and provides some of its best habitat. In 1952, trappers working rivers and streams in southwestern Wisconsin brought in beavers weighing between eighty and eighty-seven pounds. The record for the

heaviest beaver still belongs to Vernon Bailey, a mammalogist who worked for the predecessor of today's U.S. Fish and Wildlife Service. In August of 1921, Bailey trapped a beaver on the Iron River in far northern Wisconsin that tipped the scales at an amazing 110 pounds. I lived close to the Iron River for many years and had driven past it innumerable times, each time thinking about that heavyweight beaver and wondering if another record beaver was swimming in that rust-stained river.

Made For a Life in the Water

Three things set the beaver apart from other mammals: its adaptations for an aquatic life, tree-cutting activities, and the ability to modify its environment. Only humans have

Beavers attain weights up to 100 pounds.
Next pages: The beaver is well-adapted for swimming and diving.

demonstrated a greater ability to create such dramatic changes to the landscape.

Beavers are stout animals with a body that measures three to four feet from head to tail. Their bones are large for their size and they have heavy musculature. Their general size and shape are adaptations to aquatic life. A short neck, small head, and short limbs provide a streamlined shape, but beavers aren't built for speed like an otter. Instead, their compact body cuts down on heat loss to the water.

Large webbed hind feet provide propulsion, while small and delicate forelimbs are used to manipulate food objects and to carry materials while swimming. Forelimbs are held tightly against the chest while beavers swim. The hind paws are six or

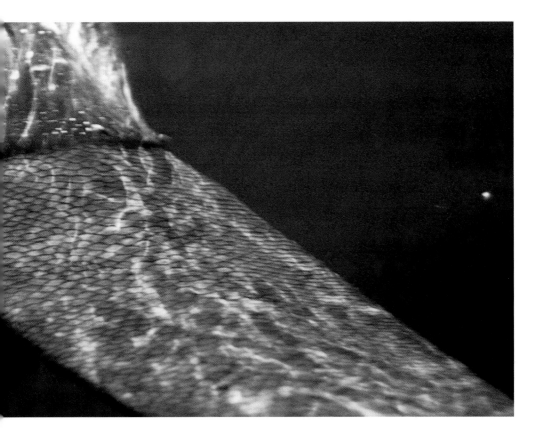

seven inches long and equally wide. Both the front and hind paws have five toes. The hind legs are longer than the front legs, giving the beaver a hunchbacked appearance while walking on land. When viewed from above, the beaver is widest at the hips tapering to the head, giving it a distinctive V-shaped look.

The beaver's toes have long, sturdy nails which serve several purposes. On the front limbs, they are used for digging and for handling food. Despite not having an opposable thumb like people, beavers can rotate a small twig while eating it, like a person eating an ear of corn. The inner two claws on each of the hind feet have split nails used for grooming. The second toe has an especially obvious split nail. Like most aquatic birds and mammals, beavers need to spend a lot of time grooming themselves so

17

Large webbed hind feet provide powerful swimming strokes.

that they remain streamlined and waterproof. The toes are used as a comb to remove tangles, mud, and parasites. A beaver has even been seen using the split nail to remove a sliver of wood lodged between its front teeth.

The most unusual and obvious physical characteristic of the beaver is the broad and flat, scaly tail. On an adult beaver, the tail typically measures between nine and fourteen inches long, between four and seven inches wide, and is about three quarters of an inch thick. The base of the tail is covered with the same kind of fur as found on the rest of the body. The flattened part of the tail, however, is covered with small scales, which superficially resemble the scales of a snake.

Almost everyone who has seen beavers in the wild knows that they use their tail to warn of danger by slapping it forcefully on the surface of the water. Other uses of the tail have been the source of much fascination, speculation, and confusion. At one time thought to be a source of propulsion while swimming, we now know that the tail is used primarily as a rudder. Early naturalists, probably working with dead specimens, thought the tail was used to carry mud and stones to be used on dams and lodges. That, too, is a myth, although the tail is used to help balance a beaver standing upright on its hind legs while gnawing on trees. For a time, the tail caused scholars to believe the beaver to be more akin to fish than to mammals. In fact, during the Middle Ages, beavers were an acceptable food during Lent because of their scaly tails.

The tail has a network of minute blood vessels throughout and a countercurrent heat exchange system of arteries and veins at its base. These specialized circulatory characteristics help the beaver dissipate extra body heat during hot weather and conserve body heat during very cold weather.

Beavers have small eyes and ears. The ears are barely obvious as small protuberances from the back of the head. The nostrils open to the side instead of to the front. Both the ears and nostrils are valvular, allowing them to be closed while swimming underwater. The eyes are guarded by a clear nictitating membrane, which closes over the eyeball when a beaver is in the water.

Beavers do not have a well developed sense of sight. They

rely more on their hearing (despite the small size of their ears) and on their sense of smell. The auditory canal of beavers is large and they are able to hear well both in and out of the water. Beavers use their noses to confirm what their eyes see and their ears hear. An unfamiliar object in a beaver pond detected by sight is usually circled while the nose is held above the water. If an animal is heard on the shore, a beaver will often swim toward it and try to get downwind so it can identify the visitor as harmless or dangerous.

During my study of beavers on the Rio Grande, I would often rise well before dawn and wade down to a stretch of river

19

The broad, scaly tail is the beaver's most unusual characteristic.

occupied by a beaver colony. Standing in waist-deep water along the river bank, I was almost invisible to the beavers emerging from their bank dens in the predawn light. They would go about their business as if I wasn't there until I moved or made a sound. Then, they would quickly circle or swim downwind from me until they picked up my scent. If I remained perfectly still and quiet, I might not be discovered until a beaver chanced to catch my scent. Despite not seeing or hearing me, my smell confirmed potential danger and a beaver would slap its tail and the family would disappear.

Similar to other animals that spend much of their lives underwater, beavers have adaptations allowing them to stay submerged for long periods of time. Like muskrats, beavers have flaps on the insides of their mouths which close over the mouth behind the incisors. This adaptation allows beavers to swim underwater carrying small sticks and to chew wood without getting water or wood splinters in their mouths.

Observers have timed beaver dives between three and ten minutes and beavers are reputed to be able to swim up to a half mile underwater. A beaver has a small heart, not surprising for an animal with a relatively slow lifestyle and in which extended periods of great exertion are rare.

Its lungs are not excessively large for its size, so it relies on its abilities to manage its supply of oxygenated blood. When it dives, a beaver's heartbeat slows and veins and arteries in the legs constrict so that less blood goes to those limbs and more is retained in the brain. The respiratory system can withstand greater amounts of carbon dioxide than other mammals. When a beaver comes up for air, it exchanges the air in its lungs far more completely than do land-dwellers. Up to seventy-five percent of the air is replaced, easily two or three times as much as a person replaces.

Flaps on the sides of the mouth allow beavers
to chew wood underwater.

An Award-Winning Smile

A person seeing a beaver for the first time can't help but be struck by its orange "buck teeth." The pair of long incisors on the top and bottom are what allow beavers to chew through the toughest woody material. The orange color comes from a hard enamel plate on the surface of the teeth. The teeth grow throughout the animal's life and are worn down and sharpened when trees are cut down. If a beaver is not allowed to chew on wood, the teeth will grow in a curved fashion, eventually preventing feeding and occasionally causing damage to the mouth.

Beavers lack the sharp canine cutting teeth of most predators. They do, however, have a complement of molars for grinding

22

Beavers must chew wood regularly to keep
their front teeth worn down.

plant material. These large ridged teeth don't seem to wear down and retain their grinding ability regardless of the animal's age.

The roots of the cutting teeth sit far back in the upper and lower jaws. Enormous pressure is exacted on the teeth and the jaws when a beaver gnaws on a tree. The pressure is greatest precisely where the large chewing muscles attach to the jaws, resulting in a lever effect which increases the biting force. The strength of this force is recognized by trappers, other people who handle live beavers, and by potential predators.

Fur Fit for Royalty

While the various physical characteristics of beaver are intriguing, the beaver's fur has been the source of greatest interest. It was the desire for rich, luxurious beaver pelts that drove trappers to explore the far reaches of North America. Beaver fur was in high demand in Europe and was worn by common folk and royalty alike. Felt hats known as "beavers" were the rage in men's fashion. Beaver pelts were an early form of currency in the wilds of North America and were traded for virtually all other goods.

Beaver fur is so thick that when it is well groomed, water rarely touches the skin. The fur is comprised of a dense layer of underfur and a sparser layer of long guard hairs. The guard hairs are ten times the diameter of the underfur hairs, creating a coarse look. Guard hairs grow up to two inches long and are longest and densest on the back. Underfur hairs which grow to about an inch long are also longest on the back, but are denser on the belly (over 100,000 hairs per square inch) than on the back (over 50,000 per square inch). The underfur hairs have a wavy texture which give the pelt an almost downy softness when it is dry.

Fur color varies a great deal both on individual beavers and among beavers in an area. Generally, beaver fur is chestnut to dark brown. In far northern latitudes, the fur can be almost black. Reddish and yellow-brown colorations occur, but are far less common.

On an individual beaver, the darkest fur is on the back. The fur on the sides, belly, and face is typically lighter. Light gray felt hats sometimes are advertised as "silver belly beavers" indicating that they are made from the dense and light hairs found on the beaver's abdomen.

While the beaver's fur has always been the primary interest for people, the scent glands located near the tail contain a substance that has been used throughout history as a base for perfumes, a lure for trappers, and in the Middle Ages as a "wonder cure," and an effective stimulus for sexual potency. The beaver uses the oily substance for waterproofing its fur and for scent marking. People used the substance known as "castoreum" as a cure for colic, rheumatism, arthritis, pleurisy, and sexual impotence. More commonly, it is still used as a base for expensive perfume because of its ability to retain any fragrance combined with it and to slowly release the aroma as it is warmed on the body. Today, castoreum is used primarily by trappers to lure beavers and other animals which are also attracted by its scent.

Beavers squeeze oil from glands near the tail for grooming.

Beavers rarely walk on two legs, but do so when
carrying mud to put on their lodges.

Origins and History

Mammals have evolved into a variety of forms and have taken on different lifestyles. Beavers are the rodents most specialized for life in the water. They are most closely related to squirrels because of a similarity in leg bones, as opposed to muskrats or nutrias which they superficially resemble in form and habits.

Classification

Beavers have their own family known as Castoridae in which they are the only members. The Castoridae family has only one surviving genus, *Castor*, and two species, *Castor canadensis*, the North American beaver, and *Castor fiber*, the European or River beaver. Fossil evidence suggests other genera and species of beaver once existed but are now extinct. There may have been as many as ten different species of beavers at one time. Most of them probably disappeared before humans came to North America, although one giant form survived up to ten thousand years ago.

Taxonomists classified North American beavers into twenty-

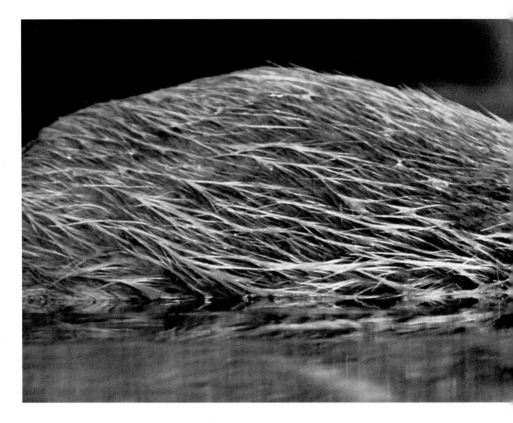

five distinct subspecies, although few of them would be distinguishable by external features. Their broad distribution across the continent and the variety of habitats they occupied no doubt allowed minor differences to be developed. Although some subspecies were probably kept separate by geographical barriers, interbreeding was possible. The decimation of beaver populations continent-wide in the 1800s and the subsequent efforts to restore their numbers and distribution in the 1900s led to a mixing of the subspecies. It is unlikely that "pure" forms of the subspecies survive today.

Despite the absence of pure races of beavers today, it is interesting to look at the historical distribution and characteristics of some of the subspecies. *Castor canadensis canadensis* was considered to be the "typical" beaver. It was the subspecies that inhabit-

ed almost all of the forested region of Canada where beavers were
most abundant. The woods beaver of Michigan, *Castor canadensis
michiganensis*, had some of the darkest fur which was extremely
valuable. One subspecies had almost blond fur and was known as
the golden beaver, *Castor canadensis subauratus*. It lived in the
San Joaquin, King, and Sacramento rivers of central California.

Some of the subspecies were probably geographically isolated
from other subspecies. They occupied river drainages in western
mountain ranges which were separated from other habitable areas
by deserts or grasslands. The only connections between these
areas were large, slow-moving rivers like the Colorado and the
Missouri. Other subspecies lived on oceanic islands off the Pacific
and Atlantic coasts such as the subspecies on Newfoundland,
Admiralty Island, and Vancouver Island.

29

The hunched back form and large size distinguishes
a beaver from a muskrat.

I became familiar with the Mexican beaver, *Castor canadensis mexicanus*, which occupied the Rio Grande and its drainages in southwestern Texas and northern Mexico. The Mexican beaver occupies the southwesternmost limit of beaver range in North America and is subjected to some of the harshest environmental conditions facing beavers. The Rio Grande flows through what is left of the short grass prairie in western Texas and into the Chihuahuan Desert on the Texas-Mexico border. The river and its floodplain form a narrow green ribbon of forest through a hot and dry no-man's land.

Mexican beavers are smaller than their northern cousins with less dense and lighter colored fur. Their small size is likely an adaptation to the warm climate of the lower Rio Grande Valley where temperatures rarely drop to freezing. Their habits differ considerably from beavers in other areas, but that will be explored later in the book.

The beaver came to have the Latin name *Castor* because of the similarity between the sexes and the because early naturalists in the Middle Ages examining the mating organs noted that a male organ seemed to be missing, at least externally. Thus, male beavers had the appearance of being castrated and the name *Castor* stuck and is still used today. The name "beaver" has its origins in an old Anglo-Saxon word, *"beofor."*

The Beaver in Legend

Any animal as curious and abundant as the beaver had to play an important role in folk legends. Beavers were present in pictographs from early human cultures and the Egyptians depicted them in their hieroglyphics. The fascination of Europeans with beavers during the Middle Ages has already been mentioned. The beaver was known to be a sacrificial animal of Germans, Finns, and Norwegians.

Beavers represented a variety of roles in North American Indian cultures. Cherokee and other eastern tribes thought the beaver had created the earth at the direction of the Creator or

Great Spirit. The earth had been covered by water until the Creator sent beavers diving to the bottom to carry mud to the surface to form dry land.

Western tribes saw beavers a little differently. The Flathead Indians believed that beavers were a race of disgraced Indians who had been changed from their human form by the Great Spirit. They worked laboriously cutting trees and building dams and lodges as atonement for their misdeeds. The Flathead believed that beavers would eventually be returned to human form after working long enough. Crow Indians thought that they would come back to earth as beavers after they died, and so believed that beavers they saw might be old relatives or friends. Some tribes viewed beavers as close brethren and chose not to kill them. Cree Indians sometimes presented a young beaver kit to a woman who had lost an infant to death.

The Ojibway or Chippewa Indians of the upper Great Lakes

31

Many activities, such as peeling bark, occur underwater.

Large trees require days and weeks of cutting;
many are abandoned before they are felled.

states believed in the beaver Creation story. Some of the bands along Lake Superior also believe that the beaver was responsible in part for the shape of the land. One particular story accounts for Chequamegon Bay in northern Wisconsin and the Apostle Islands which lay at its north end. The legend is told that the Great Spirit wanted to keep the beaver captive and so created the bay with a barrier across it to pen the beaver in. But the beaver broke through the barrier and started to swim out into Lake Superior. The Great Spirit was so angry that he took huge handfuls of mud and threw them at the beaver as it swam away. Each of the throws of mud created a new island now known collectively as the Apostle Islands.

The Giant Beaver

Imagine yourself in a small band of human hunters ten to twelve thousand years ago. You are walking along a river bank in what is now Ohio only several hundred miles south of a lobe of the huge glacier covering much of northern North America. The river is melt water from the glacier which is just beginning to recede. The river's floodplain is sparsely forested with willow and aspen trees.

There are signs of a large animal's presence. Every few hundred yards, grasses and sedges are matted down where the animal walked and dragged itself from the river to a small copse of trees. Gnawed stumps indicate that the animal bit through trees a half-foot in diameter and hewed out huge chips of larger trees. The animal apparently dragged the largest of trees to the water's edge where it ate the leaves and small twigs and peeled the soft bark off small branches.

There are legends told by your clan of a rarely seen, giant, tree-cutting, furry animal with enormous teeth and a large flat tail that makes the sound of a thunderclap when struck against the water. The animal swims and dives in rivers and lakes and sometimes stays underwater so long that it has swum out of sight before it comes up for air. It is told that the Creator asked this

33

Next pages: The modern-day beaver would have been dwarfed by the now extinct 500-pound giant beaver.

animal to dive to the bottom of the watery world to bring up the
first earth from which all land originated.

You have never seen this animal, which is thought to be van-
ishing from the world, but have observed its much smaller cousin
many times. You have begun to question if the animal ever existed except as a mythical creature in stories told to scare children.
Then, you come around a bend in the river and a huge dark
brown animal on the bank awkwardly launches itself into the
water and sends a cascade of spray skyward with a slap of its tail.
The size of the animal and the sound it makes stops everyone in
your small party in their tracks. A pungent musky aroma pervades
the air. It is true! The Creator really did make a giant tree-cutter!
Mumblings of prayers to the Creator are mixed with excited talk

36

A beaver's ears become especially visible
when it is alert for danger.

of how the animal might provide food for the clan for several weeks if it only could be caught on land and killed . . .

Long before primitive humans wandered the globe and after the fall of dinosaurs, some thirty-five million years ago, a distant ancestor of present-day squirrels and beavers gave rise to a variety of forms of small mammals which used their large front teeth to gnaw on nuts, seeds, and woody vegetation. Over the course of millions of years, evolutionary forces created several species of semi-aquatic animals which specialized in eating bark from trees. One of these species followed a path toward gigantism as was the case for other lines of animals, notably bears, cats, dogs, and elephants. This giant form of beaver, known as *Castoroides*, pushed its range to the far North where its large size was an advantage in cold climates.

Castoroides, the giant beaver, is an intriguing mystery to scientists studying ancient extinct mammals. Although it is not the ancestor of modern beavers, it coexisted with them and other now extinct small and medium-sized species of beavers in North America until about ten thousand years ago, when it and other giant mammals quickly went extinct. Its fossilized remains have been unearthed from places in North America just south of the extent of glaciers.

Castoroides was a strictly North American species although it appeared to have a giant cousin, *Trogontherium*, which wandered northern Europe and Asia and coexisted with the smaller beavers living there. Fossil collections suggest that *Castoroides* was most abundant in Indiana when it was more of a boreal forest and less of a prairie. It is not clear when *Castoroides* originated. It lived through the various advances and retreats of glaciers, but was unable to survive the changes occurring after the last glacial retreat. While there is no evidence for the cause of its extinction, it is probably far more than coincidence that its extinction occurred during the period when humans first appeared in North America. The rapid disappearance of *Castoroides* and other giant mammals, such as woolly mammoths, may have been caused in large part by highly mobile and efficient human hunters.

Smaller and far more abundant than *Castoroides*, the

Canadian beaver, *Castor canadensis*, flourished during the period when its giant cousin went extinct. The first fossils of species of *Castor* are from Germany and China, from a period starting two to five million years ago in a time period called the Pliocene when many of the modern species of birds and mammals first appeared. Today's two species of beavers probably evolved from a common Eurasian ancestor. *Castor canadensis* and *Castor fiber* are so closely related, in fact, that they can successfully interbreed.

The first human to see a giant beaver must have been amazed, especially if the more common smaller beaver was seen first. Even I have trouble imagining a beaver that weighed over five hundred pounds, the weight of a large black bear. Giant beavers stretched over five feet long from head to tail and its back would have come well above your knee when it was on all fours. Its skull was twelve inches long with six-inch incisors, compared with the five-inch skull and one-inch incisors of today's beaver.

Unfortunately, we have very little idea what kind of lifestyle giant beavers led. We don't know exactly what they ate or who ate them, whether or not they constructed dams and lodges, how long they lived, or what their young were like. Scientists believe that *Castoroides* was even more highly specialized than modern beavers. It had great difficulty moving its enormous bulk around on land and probably rarely wandered very far from the water where it was vulnerable to predation by humans and other large predators, like saber-toothed cats and dire wolves.

While the day of the giant beaver has come and gone, we are fortunate to be in the presence of its smaller cousin, which is truly remarkable on its own part. The history of the beaver and its way of life is a fascinating saga.

Flaps close ears and nose to keep water out.

The lodge is the focal point of a beaver colony.

C h a p t e r   3

A Place to Call Home

The only constants that can be used to describe beaver habitat are water and trees. Just about everything else varies a great deal, and even the kinds of water and trees can be quite different. This shouldn't be all that unexpected for a creature that inhabits areas from the Arctic Circle to the Gulf of Mexico and from the desert Southwest to the Maine north woods. The ability to survive across a range of environmental conditions is a testament to the flexibility of the habits of beavers and their advantage over other creatures in being able to modify their environment for their own good.

The heart of beaver range in North America is in the aspen dominated forests of the Great Lake states and southern Canada. There, they find their favorite foods and a myriad of lakes, rivers, streams, and other wetlands. In the headwaters area of the Mississippi River in north-central Minnesota, there exists an enormous complex of freshwater habitats of all kinds and sizes. It is not nearly as well known as the Everglades of Florida, but is equally impressive in its own right. In virtually every pond, lake, river, and stream, there is a family of beavers. This area probably holds one of the densest concentrations of beavers in the world.

Excellent habitat for beavers also exists in New England and parts of eastern Canada. High mountain streams of the Rocky Mountains are what come to mind when many people think of "classic" beaver habitat. While many beavers find the mile-high elevation to their liking, the steep, fast-running streams present a challenge to beavers trying to create a stable environment. Similar conditions along the Pacific Northwest coast limit the success of beavers, but they have figured out ways to survive there as well.

The central part of the eastern United States is good, but not excellent, habitat for beavers. There are a limited number of lakes, but a wealth of rivers and streams. The slow-moving, murky rivers and wetlands of the Southeast are surprisingly good

42

beaver habitat. Although it doesn't conjure up the romantic notion of mountain men trapping beaver in cold, clear streams, the Southeast has more than its share of beavers, particularly those which have adapted to the river life.

Perhaps the most surprising habitat exploited by beavers is the remote web of large rivers and their tributaries in the desert Southwest. A person on a raft trip through the Grand Canyon or floating a stretch of the Rio Grande in Big Bend National Park is in far better beaver habitat than they might think. While beavers occupying these large rivers generally don't build dams or lodges, they find a way to eke out a living in the cool floodplains where the adjacent desert may be only a few yards away.

Beavers were one of the keys to the exploration and settle-

43

Beavers create excellent habitat for other animals,
such as the moose.

Beavers travel inland away from water
to find trees for food.

ment of the North American wilderness, but they are not creatures that require solitude to survive. In fact, beavers and people
live remarkably close together in many areas. Man-made ponds
sometimes support a family or a transient beaver passing
through, especially if they are connected to a stream or river
system by a drainage ditch. Roadside ditches have become commonly used habitat for beavers unable to compete successfully
for the prime habitats.

A stream flowing through a farmer's field in central Michigan
may support a beaver family if there is a nearby woodlot or trees
along the stream bank. A small lake in Ontario ringed with summer homes may also have a beaver colony with different designs
on the trees planted and cared for in the lakeshore yards of the
human residents. Irrigation ditches in Tennessee might suit a
bachelor beaver just fine for a time while he is looking for a better place to start a home and family.

And often, what doesn't look like potential beaver habitat to
us can look surprisingly good after a dam is built to raise the
water level and after a series of canals are dug to reach the nearby
trees. Leave it to the beavers to turn a low-rent district into high-
priced real estate on the beaver market.

Beavers can turn a grove of aspen into a meadow
in just a few weeks.

Nature's Lumberjack

Of all of the physical and behavioral attributes, the beaver is best known for its ability to cut down trees. Tree-cutting serves two purposes—acquisition of food, and material for use in building dams and lodges.

The front teeth, skull, and muscles associated with the jaws and neck are well-suited for the pressure needed to cut through wood. Beavers have learned to be extremely efficient in their cutting methods as well, although they often seem to cut in nonsensical patterns.

Felling Trees

Typically, one beaver works alone on a tree. Occasionally, it is joined by one other. Paintings and drawings by early naturalists often depict an entire beaver colony working together on the tree or working in an assembly line fashion. Some of the beavers are cutting a tree, others are cutting off the small branches, still others are dragging the tree to the water, and the rest are swimming the tree to the lodge or dam where more beavers are performing construction work. This idealistic notion no doubt reflects the

Next pages: Trees cut by beavers may fall in any direction.

perception of efficiency in Nature and forethought by animals
other than humans. Observations by scientists have proven that
beavers don't set up such an elaborate work system.

Tree-cutting can take anywhere between a few seconds to
hours or days of work. The beavers I studied in West Texas primarily felled very small trees, seedlings and small saplings,
because they were cutting them only for food. The one- to two-
inch-diameter trees came down with just a few bites that went
through the entire stem. Smaller seedlings came down with just
one bite.

50

Beavers use powerful jaw muscles to rip
chips of wood out of a tree.

When a tree is over three inches in diameter, beavers can't bite straight through so they cut chips out of the trunk, much as a lumberjack would cut wedges out with an ax. The beaver bites down with its front teeth and rips the chip out when it is cut almost through. It typically works around the tree, but sometimes cuts from just one side. A person who examines an area where beavers have been actively cutting trees notices that there are a variety of cutting patterns, perhaps reflecting the individual styles of each beaver.

Very small trees are usually felled by the beaver while it is on all four feet. Most of the "mini-stumps" I found in my study area were within an inch or two of the ground. When a beaver works on a larger tree, it stands on its hind legs and uses its tail as a brace. The forearms hold the tree and the head is angled to the side instead of straight upright.

On small trees with succulent bark near the base, a beaver may tear strips of bark off the tree and eat them before starting to cut out woody chips. On larger trees with corky bark, bark and chips are cut immediately.

The width of the cut depends on the size of the tree. Beavers work on the top of the cut for a while tearing out a few chips, then move to the bottom and do the same. After a time, they move around the tree and tend to keep a fairly even width and depth. In my years of travel in beaver country, I have been amazed by how precisely some of the cuts have been made.

I have also observed cutting activity on a large tree that was discontinued for some unknown reason. Occasionally, I find a tree still standing with only a core of two or three inches holding the tree in place. The width of the cut is within a fraction of an inch of being even all the way around and the depth of the cut looks as though a master woodcraftsman had made it.

Trees smaller than six inches in diameter can be felled in fifteen minutes or less depending on how soft the wood is and how large and experienced the beaver doing the work is. Those who have studied beavers, many trappers, and other outdoorspeople, have seen what we think must have been the largest tree ever cut by a beaver. Scientific journals don't regularly report such information and the tales of casual observers tend to be slightly exaggerated. However, a few accounts in reputable journals report trees three feet or slightly over in diameter that have been felled by a beaver. Trees of that size may take a few hours of cutting per night over the course of days or weeks. Sometimes, these trees are right next to much smaller trees that would appear to be easier work. It's hard to guess why a beaver would tackle such large one, especially when it is obviously too big to drag away.

Beavers have been given far too much credit for being able to size up the configuration of a tree's crown, its lean, and the probability of a cut tree hanging up in the surrounding trees. In fact, many trees may fall toward the water simply because of the slope, while other trees lay jackstrawed on the ground. Some trees never even make it to the ground and are hung up in their neighbors.

When a tree felled by beavers gets hung up in another tree, the beavers will not cut the supporting tree. Instead, they leave it there or try to further cut the leaning tree. Occasionally, beavers will climb up a tree that is leaning over to sever some of the lower branches. I saw evidence of this on the floodplain of the Rio Grande where a cottonwood tree had been cut and felled by beaver, but was hung up in another tree's crown. Beavers had apparently climbed the leaning tree because there were fresh cuts of some of the lower branches. The beaver doing the cutting must have had good balance and no fear of heights as the cut branches were a good fifteen feet above the ground. How it got down after climbing up I have no idea.

As is the case for human loggers, tree felling is a dangerous occupation for beavers. Although a beaver can, no doubt, feel a tree starting to give way and can usually rush away to safety, once in a while, a tree falls on the animal pinning it to the ground or killing it instantly. I have seen photographs of dead beavers which had been trapped under trees. If not killed right away, they struggle to pull free as evidenced by the digging and clawing at the ground.

Once a tree is on the ground, the next order of business is to cut smaller branches with succulent bark, leaves, and buds from the top of the tree. Here is where other members of the colony may join in with the animal that felled the tree. After

small branches are cut, larger branches may be cut in manageable lengths which can be carried in the water and used on the dam or lodge.

Just how beavers carry large branches back to the water has been the source of sometimes wild speculation. One of the more amusing accounts comes from Polish naturalist G. Schotti, who in 1662 wrote a short description of the beaver and its habits. He wrote that branches were conveyed from the places they were cut to the dam or lodge by beavers piling up a stack of branches between the legs of an old beaver or one that couldn't work for other reasons. The old beaver was turned on its back and dragged

Once a tree is felled, a beaver starts to
cut the small branches.

by the tail to the water while it held onto the branches. He reasoned that this accounted for why some beaver hunters took beavers that had hairless backs.

While this account is creative and amusing, a beaver actually works singly and grabs the butt end of a branch in its mouth and drags it to the side. Well worn paths between the water and the cutting area are evidence of the repeated dragging that takes place after a tree has been cut down. Some of these paths are used over the course of an entire ice-free season and may be worn a foot or deeper into the earth. On the Rio Grande, where there were often wide sandbars between the river and the forest, I watched for signs of drag marks at the water's edge and followed the marks back to the forest and into the trees. The beavers were sometimes dragging branches and small trees fifty or more yards from the interior forest to the edge, and then another one or two hundred feet across the widest sandbars, a testament to their powerful jaws, necks, and legs—and to their persistence.

All in all, Nature's lumberjack is an efficient, if not perfect, tree-feller. Unlike their human counterparts, however, they are feller, limber, skidder, and debarker all in one.

Dens and Lodges

More than any other animal, save humans, beavers are able to modify their environment to serve their own needs. Their ability to build complex structures, establish travel networks, and manipulate water levels is unparalleled.

Beavers live either in a den in the earth or in a lodge constructed of branches and mud. Lodges are preferred housing in all situations, but sometimes are not feasible to construct. Beavers living along large rivers which flood frequently or in areas where there are few trees live in bank dens.

Bank dens, or burrows as they are sometimes called, are constructed by digging into the bank with the forepaws and kicking dirt out with the back feet. Den entrances are underwater and the tunnel is dug at a slightly upward angle until it is above water

level. Then, a larger chamber is hollowed out of the bank. The chambers are sometimes associated with a tangle of tree roots which provide additional stability to the living quarters.

Burrows vary in length. I found some on the Rio Grande which were just six feet back into the bank. Others continue twenty or thirty feet into the bank before opening into the living chamber. The chambers also vary in size. Bank burrows built by bachelor beavers are small. Families living in bank burrows year-round sometimes construct several large chambers at the end of the same tunnel.

Beavers living in lodges usually have several bank dens in the colony. They get used as high water or low water refuges and also are places to hide away from the lodge. Their most creative use is as air pockets during the winter. Beavers swimming under the ice can lengthen their time away from the lodge by swimming to a bank den to get a fresh breath of air. Beavers also breathe from air

A beaver lodge can be six feet high and thirty feet across.
Next pages: Beavers collect mud from the bottom
of the pond to put on the lodge.

pockets trapped under the ice. They also have been observed exhaling the air from their lungs, allowing it to rise to the ice in a bubble, and then reinhaling it—the bubble presumably containing new oxygen gained by passing through the water.

Lodges may be the final step on the evolutionary ladder of housing development for beavers. Watching the process of lodge building reveals that preliminary steps are identical to those of burrow excavation. The differences are that the tunnel is cut through the surface of the ground and that sticks and mud are added to the top.

New lodge construction can occur at any time during the ice-free season as beavers establish new colonies. However, beavers in established colonies begin to build new lodges and maintain old lodges in the late summer and early fall.

Most colonies have several lodges in various degrees of repair. One is clearly the main lodge to be used in the winter, but all of them may receive a little home improvement now and then. New lodges are built to take advantage of a small movement in the activity center of the colony or to replace a damaged lodge or one that is no longer inhabitable.

Once a tunnel has been constructed and has broken through to the surface, the colony members start piling sticks on top of the hole. It has been commonly thought that beavers place the sticks in a manner that creates a chamber at the bottom. However, close observations reveal no such strategy. Instead, a beaver works from the tunnel and cuts away portions of branches to create the living space.

Mud is brought in through the tunnel and piled next to the escape hole to create a low feeding platform. This is the spot where beavers entering the lodge stop to dry their fur, feed on a branch, and groom. Most lodges also have a slightly higher level which is kept dry and is often carpeted with wood shavings. The beavers sleep on the upper levels. The inside chamber of a lodge can be up to five feet across and two feet high.

Once sticks are in place on the outside of the lodge, the colony members start plastering the outside with mud. They carry the mud up under their chins with their forepaws and walk upright on their legs up the side of the lodge. Mud is poked into

An armful of mud held against the chest is destined to be used
to waterproof and insulate the lodge.

most nooks and crannies except for the top few feet. This small unplastered area serves as a vent and allows for air exchange in the lodge.

During winter, the mud freezes solid and provides adequate insulation so that the inside of the lodge is above freezing, heated exclusively by the body heat of the inhabitants. Spring and summer rains wash some of the mud off the lodges, which means steady employment for the colony every fall.

Adults do most of the work on the lodges although all age classes participate. Kits generally bring sticks to the lodge and don't carry mud. Females do a bit more lodge maintenance than males.

Single beavers also build lodges. Their lodges tend to be a little smaller, but you can't always judge the number of beavers in a lodge by its size. Nor can you judge the number of beavers in a colony by the number of lodges they maintain. Like people, some beaver families prefer more room than others.

Some of the largest beaver lodges have been found in the Great Lakes states and in eastern Canada. Heights above the water have exceeded ten feet and distances across the base have been forty to fifty feet.

There may be more than one entrance to a lodge and some lodges have more than one chamber. One well-known nature writer and photographer tried to swim into a beaver lodge by following an underwater tunnel. He got in around fifteen feet without reaching the living chamber and nearly got stuck as he tried to turn around.

Lodges found associated with the bank may appear to be islands. When a lodge is built on top of a bank tunnel, the colony may also be raising water levels with a dam. Sometimes, the rise in water level isolates the lodge from shore making it less vulnerable to potential predators. In other cases, beavers build lodges starting them away from shore. They push sticks into the mud and pile other sticks on top of them. Then, they cut out the chambers and the entrances from below.

Beaver homes range from the efficiency apartments found in bachelor beavers' bank burrows to high-rent penthouses which are the island lodges with multiple chambers. A colony usually

has several of each within their home range, alternating between them throughout the seasons and years.

D a m s

While beavers have developed abilities as lumberjacks and architects, they are best when it comes to constructing elaborate water control projects. They build dams to raise water levels and then cut canals, make plunge holes, dig underwater aqueducts, and dredge channels into the bottom of ponds.

61

An active lodge may stay snow-free in winter.

Damming the flow of moving water is the strongest instinct a beaver seems to have outside of eating and procreating. The sound of running water alone spurs a beaver to action. Beavers will dam anything from a spring to a fast-running stream. They are unable to harness the largest rivers, but are very creative in using mid-stream boulders and islands to anchor dams that span larger and faster flowing rivers than one might think possible.

Beavers, like most people, seem to desire stability in their lives. The stability they seek the most is the water level of their colony site. Lakes and most ponds provide a stable water environment and beavers rarely construct dams on them. When they do, they usually pick a spot on the outlet stream.

Rivers and streams have fluctuating water levels and also have a limited amount of safe foraging habitat. Dams built on these water bodies raise the water level so that streamside vegetation is flooded and food is accessible without leaving the water. Stabilization of the water level allows a lodge to be built along the river bank where it would otherwise be washed away.

I have seen beaver dams all over North America and can attest to the fact that they will build a dam on every body of running water on which they are physically able to do so. Dams are noticeably absent only on large rivers and steep, fast-moving streams where spring snow melt produces raging torrents.

Even though the beavers I studied on the Rio Grande could

63

Dams control water levels and make ponds out of streams.

Dams are more difficult to construct and maintain
in high mountain areas.

not get a dam across the main channel of the river, I discovered an area in Big Bend National Park next to the river where small springs created a marsh-like environment. The beavers occupying that stretch of river constructed a small dam across the area where the marsh drained into the big river. Their dam raised the water level in the marsh and allowed them to move safely to gather food.

While many people have seen beaver dams, few have observed beavers constructing or maintaining them. Beavers do most of their work at night and only dedicated researchers, trappers, and amateur naturalists have shown the patience to sit up after dark to watch Nature's engineer at work.

One of the first activities of a colony of beavers moving into a new area is to construct a dam. Most dam-building occurs in early spring and late summer, with a couple of months of intense activity in each season.

While human engineers carefully select sites for their dams so that costs are kept low, dam stability is high, and results are predictable, beavers seem to have a more haphazard approach. Some beaver dams appear to be in an ideal location while others are located in an area where they are difficult to construct and don't provide maximum benefit. In these cases, there often is a far better location nearby. Scientists believe that beavers learn through experience and that older beavers may make better selections than younger animals.

Beavers respond to both the sound and the feel of running water and often choose locations for dams that are close to places where the water is running fastest and making the most noise. On a number of trout streams I have fished in northern Wisconsin, I have found dams in places where the river had narrowed and was running noisily over exposed rocks.

Such exposed rocks may also provide a strong base for the dam. Dams are sometimes built in a curved or zig-zag fashion to take advantage of instream boulders and rocks.

Beavers typically start dam construction by pushing up a narrow ridge of mud and gravel all the way across the stream. If the current is so strong that this is impractical, they begin by anchoring sticks in the substrate. Beavers will often eat the

65

bark off small sticks before using them in the dam so no food goes to waste.

It may take a number of tries and certainly requires concerted efforts to establish the base. With the base started, they add sticks and rocks as they gradually build up the dam from the bottom. The entire dam from one side of the river to the other is raised uniformly, perhaps to keep the pressure of the running water even across the structure.

Adults initiate most dams, but are aided in construction by all but the youngest colony members. Beavers add sticks to the dam by pushing them into the existing structure using their powerful jaw and neck muscles. The result is a strong latticework. Small rocks are often pushed or carried across the pond to the dam where they are placed near the base or sometimes in the

66

Soft vegetation and mud are used in dam building.

body of the dam.

Once the dam's crest is above water level, mud is added to restrict flow through the network of sticks and rocks. The mud is usually daubed on the upstream side of the dam so that the water forces the mud into the inner crevices. Eventually, the last leaks are filled and the dam holds back almost all of the water.

As water backs up behind the dam, it floods a large area. Typically, the water finds another channel and flows past the dam to the side. In these cases, the beavers will build additional small dams to capture that water flow and to increase the efficiency of their main structure.

On slow-moving streams, a dam may be so well constructed that virtually no water escapes and the downstream section goes dry. More commonly, enough water escapes through cracks in the dam to keep the water level downstream at an acceptable level for fish and other stream creatures. Sometimes, beavers build secondary dams to back up water against the downstream side of the main dam so that the pressure of the water on the upstream side is partially counterbalanced.

Dams take on all shapes and sizes. Some are small with narrow crests that can't be walked across without getting wet feet. Others have wide, stable crests that actually serve as travelways for a variety of creatures which prefer to cross streams with dry feet.

Dams are usually fairly straight across although some are bowed downstream because the stream flow pushed material as the dam was being built. Others have an upstream curve which is a hydrologically superior design.

The desire to build dams across running water is so strong that beavers will use any material they have available. I have seen and read about beaver dams made from cornstalks when no woody building materials were nearby.

There is no register of the largest and longest beaver dams, but people who wander the woods and canoe streams and rivers bring back tales of some monsters. Trappers provide most of the examples. Some dams span hundreds of yards and a few are over ten feet tall from their base to their crest.

One might think a simple structure of sticks and mud would

not have much strength. I have learned from experience, however, that this is not the case. On several occasions I have tried to pull sticks out of dams when temporarily stalled by water backed up across a woods road. The first few sticks come out easily and water starts to flow over the crest. Sticks farther down on the dam come out with far more difficulty, if it all. Standing on the upstream side of the dam in rubber boots while pulling at sticks reminds one of how much force running water has and just how strong a dam has to be to hold it all back.

Unfortunately, I have had to continue removing sticks even after this realization, so that the force of the water itself would pull at the sticks and start to wash out the structure. This is not a safe practice, as I learned one day in northern Maine. I had driven on a woods road to get to my study site where I was conducting a loon research project. I was disappointed to find a beaver dam across a low water crossing in the road which had created a pool some six feet deep where I wanted to drive. I started to pull sticks out as I fought the black flies and no-see-ums.

The water started to flow through the first break I made so I moved to one side and started to make another breach. That break in the dam caused that side to quickly fall apart and I barely escaped back to the side where I left my truck without getting washed downstream. I thought the water level would drop quickly, but there was so much water stored behind the dam that it subsided slowly. I grew impatient and ventured out onto the dam once more to create another break. It fell apart under my weight and I stumbled into the upstream pool where I fell and got soaked, but avoided being swept away in the current by sheer luck alone.

A beaver dam is a wonder to behold, but like all structures, it requires maintenance to survive. Beavers regularly conduct inspections of their work to patch leaks and shore up weak spots. Adult males frequently conduct detailed inspections of the entire dam which may last five minutes or more. Casual inspections taking less than a minute are conducted more frequently.

The actions of humans, flood events, and the continued force of water eat away at the dam. Small holes in the dam are repaired by bringing up mud from the bottom and by pulling materials

Beaver dams are sometimes marvels of engineering.

from the sides of the breaks. Medium-sized breaks require more effort. Beavers often swim into the hole to block the flow of the water and pull branches into the hole from the sides of the break. They then back out of the hole and push mud into the hole to seal it.

Large breaks in dams require greater efforts. In these cases, new materials are brought to the dam and jammed into the sides of the break until a latticework is established. Smaller sticks, rocks and mud are added until the job is finished. All colony members may assist in the reconstruction of a breached dam when it threatens to drop water levels to an unacceptable level. The adult male and female frequently rearrange sticks placed by younger animals reinforcing the idea that beavers learn the best construction principles through experience.

70

A break in the dam brings a beaver over
for a closer look.

Most beavers typically overcompensate when there is a break. They often add materials to the crest even though water is not flowing over the top of the dam. They seem to be driven by the need to quiet the sound of running water and may build and build to the top even when the water is leaking through the middle of the dam.

On the other hand, some beavers may not repair or add to a dam even if water is pouring over its top. Apparently, these beavers try to regulate the water level to their best advantage and will not blindly add to a dam when the result will flood a lodge or den.

Beavers occasionally create holes in dams to allow some water to escape during floods or when they want to bring the water level in the pond down a bit. They typically cut a hole about the diameter of their body through the dam and repair it when the level is acceptable.

Canals, Channels, and Plunge Holes

Lodges and dams are the most obvious structures built by beavers. Less well known, yet equally magnificent in their own right are the series of canals, channels, and plunge holes built in some beaver colonies.

Beavers like to create a network of regular travelways to aid in their movement underwater and on land. Most beaver ponds have at least one shallow channel cut into the bottom substrate and many have a complex network.

The channels generally are extensions from the lodge entrances to heavily used areas such as food caches, dams, and feeding or scent marking activity areas. From above, they resemble a spider web of channels across the bottom of the pond. The channels serve as underwater route markers, particularly in iron-stained waters with poor visibility. Additionally, they lend more depth to the pond when ice freezes thick. Beavers dredge these channels frequently, much like humans dredge shipping channels to keep them open and usable.

Some beaver colonies construct canals on land to extend the safety of their waterways inland to feeding sites. The canals I have seen have been in colonies associated with sphagnum bogs where the soil is soft and easy to excavate. People who have watched beavers building canals report that they dig at the earth with their forepaws and push the materials to the sides with their paws and shoulders. Rocks are picked out and pushed aside and roots are chewed off.

Some canals connect nearby ponds, others just extend ponds inland. They may extend a pond to a small spring which partially fills the canal with water. When beavers occupy bogs, they cut canals across the bog so that they don't have to swim around the outside open water section.

People have discovered underground canals and plunge holes quite by accident. For me, it was in a northern Maine cedar swamp near Millinocket Lake. The swamp bordered a lake I wanted to walk around and as I walked, I noticed some above-ground canals created by beavers. Suddenly, without warning, I fell through what looked like stable ground into a canal beavers had excavated from the lake edge some fifty yards into the forest.

I escaped without any broken bones, but with a twisted ankle. Curious to see where the canal went, I followed what I thought was its direction until I found a plunge hole providing the inland entrance. The plunge hole was a small seep which kept a few inches of water in the bottom of the canal. Not surprisingly, only a few yards from the plunge hole was a small grove of aspen trees growing on a slightly elevated knob of dry land in the cedar swamp. Further inspection revealed recent cutting activity. These innovative and apparently hungry beavers found this isolated grove which wasn't visible from the lake and created the canal to provide a safer way to access it.

Beavers construct canals to provide safe inland travel routes.

Winter food comes from sticks cached underwater
and brought to the lodge or shoreline to eat.

Food Habits

An animal weighing fifty or more pounds, spending much of its time in the water, and sometimes living in cold climates, needs a lot of calories to keep its internal engine running. The beaver, unfortunately, doesn't have easily digestible, high-calorie options on its menu. Instead, it must eat vegetation containing high amounts of cellulose, which is notoriously difficult to digest and from which to extract calories.

The beaver makes up for calorie-poor food by choosing from its limited menu carefully and by eating and eating and eating.

Beavers and their food habits have been studied all over North America and Europe. Researchers have documented the use of hundreds of different kinds of plants. In just one study of beavers in Alabama, Master's student Philip Wilkinson listed fifty-three species of trees and non-woody plants used by beaver over just one-and-a-half years of study.

Tree bark is the primary food of beavers throughout most of their range during the fall and winter. Leaves, twigs, and buds are used during the spring and summer. Spring and summer also provide a great variety of herbaceous plants which are far more easy to digest than bark. Thus, summer does not provide a great challenge for acquiring nutritional foods because many soft plants

75

Next pages: Leaves and soft plants are
preferred summer fare.

grow in and along lakes, rivers, and streams.

With such a variety of plants to choose from in any one area and an equally diverse range across North America, it is difficult to identify favored summer foods. However, some that are used commonly include cattail, arrowhead, pondweed, smartweed, milfoil, pond lily and a variety of sedges. Beavers are particularly fond of the starchy roots of cattails and pond lilies. They also sample some seemingly less likely fare including nettles, blackberry, and the gritty stems of bulrushes.

During the summer months, I noticed beavers on the Rio Grande digging at riverbanks where sedges were growing. They left the above-ground stems, but ate the roots. Similarly, they ate the roots of species of reeds or canes which grew in thick stands along most of the river. Beavers have been noticed dining on large mats of algae or pond scum which they swim into and pull together with their forepaws. Although it didn't occur to me when I observed it, other biologists have likened it to the eating of spaghetti.

Beavers will eat herbaceous vegetation as long as it is available into the autumn. This varies, of course, across their range. In the North, herbaceous plants are available for just a month or two. On the southern end of the range, herbaceous plants may be available for over half the year. Some colonies even survive the winter by digging up and eating the rhizomes and tubers of pond lilies. Eventually, however, in most colonies beavers turn their attention to trees.

Bark is not a highly nutritious food because it contains a number of chemicals designed to repel potential diners. As a tree gets older, its bark on the trunk and the larger branches becomes cork-like in texture. Beavers prefer the thin, smooth bark growing on seedlings, saplings, and the small branches of large trees. When saplings are available, beavers prefer to cut them down and eat their bark. Large trees are cut down to get at the small branches. Not surprisingly, only when food becomes scarce in an area will bark from large branches and the trunk be eaten.

Dozens of species of trees grow in riparian areas in North America. Yet the beaver is well known for its affinity for just a handful. Whenever they are present, aspens, cottonwoods, and

willows are the preferred foods. Maples, alder, and sweet gum are frequently reported to be commonly used as well.

Aspen, cottonwood, and willow are pioneer species which readily recolonize burned over, logged, or flooded areas and they are abundant in many riparian and adjacent areas. They also respond to being cut down by resprouting from the roots. In many ways, they are ideal beaver foods. Aspen bark is particularly nutritious because some photosynthesis takes place in the bark as well as in the leaves. Eventually, however, repeated cutting kills the plant and beavers are forced to eat less favored foods or to move on to a different area.

Across the Upper Midwest where aspen is common, I have seen thousands of acres of forest next to lakeshores and rivers in which beavers have selectively felled the aspen trees leaving only

79

Aspen trees are a beaver's favorite food
wherever they are found.

the pines and birches. The areas inevitably become choked with hazel brush which apparently doesn't compare favorably for the beaver's palate.

Aspen, being primarily a northern or high elevation tree, was absent from my study area on the Rio Grande. Several species of willow grew fairly commonly in isolated patches along the floodplain. Cottonwood, which had once been common, was very rare, having been replaced by an aggressive exotic species called tamarisk or salt cedar. Beavers there ate willow most frequently. In fact, every willow stand on the river had a beaver colony associated with it.

80

The remaining cottonwoods were mostly large, old trees growing a hundred yards or more back from the river. There weren't nearly enough of them in any one area to support a beaver colony for very long. Because they were so far back from the river's edge, it was dangerous for beavers to walk to them and spend time gnawing at their large trunks. However, during floods which reduced the distance between the water and the cottonwoods, I found signs of fresh chewing at most of the sites. I took this as an indication that beavers preferred cottonwoods over willows, but wouldn't risk predation to cut them down unless they were close to the water's edge.

81

Tree stems are often cut to manageable lengths
before being dragged into the water.

In areas where aspens, cottonwoods, or willows, are not available, beavers turn to other trees. They generally avoid pines and other softwoods which have sticky resins in their bark, but they do occasionally show up on the food list from research studies. Oaks and other hardwood trees seem to be starvation foods.

It is always risky to attribute the felling of trees to food because trees are also used to make lodges and dams. However, on the Rio Grande, where neither dams nor lodges were built, every tree that was cut down was probably used for food. Tamarisk was the only softwood there and it was used only when willows were scarce and then, only small seedlings and saplings were cut down. Tamarisk is a species that has been in the area less than a hundred years, indicating the beaver's ability to adapt to a new food.

I found beavers felling a dozen or so tree species, one of which would have been the last on my list had I been predicting. In one beaver colony near the town of Boquillas, Mexico, I

82

A beaver's powerful jaws can cut through a
small tree or branch in just a few bites.

discovered beavers cutting down and peeling the bark off a tree called "catclaw acacia," so named because of the long, sturdy thorns growing on its trunk and branches. The thorns looked as if they had been neatly clipped off, probably with a quick (and careful!) nip of the incisors.

D i g e s t i o n

Like all animals that eat green or woody vegetation, beavers have evolved a digestive system to deal with the high amounts of cellulose. Many animals that eat vegetation are large-bodied and have large stomachs and intestines providing for slow processing of the food. Beavers do not have exceptionally large stomachs. However, they do have a large pouched digestive organ called a cecum, and a cardiogastric gland, a somewhat unique organ which produces highly acidic juices that drain into the stomach. Only koalas and wombats, two other mammals about the size of beavers which have a vegetarian diet, have a similar gland.

Beavers make use of foods with lots of cellulose using two adaptations—bacteria in their cecum and the reingestion of their feces. The bacteria allow beavers to break down about one third of the cellulose in a meal which stays in the digestive tract for at least a couple of days. Beavers then capture some of the remaining cellulose by sending it through the system again.

Beavers reingest some of their feces to give the digestive system another chance at breaking down more cellulose. Although not commonly observed, reingestion of feces is fairly common among small mammals that eat a lot of vegetation.

A fairly inefficient digestive system and some foods that aren't all that nutritious means that a beaver has to eat a lot. Captive beavers have maintained weight on one-and-a-half to two pounds of aspen bark a day. A typical one-inch-diameter aspen tree, which takes five or six years to grow, has about three pounds of bark on it. An acre of aspen trees this size produces about three tons of bark or enough to feed a large colony of ten beavers for about a year.

Winter Caches

Beavers living in northern latitudes where ice covers their ponds for more than a few days or weeks have to adapt their food gathering habits. Like other rodents, they have learned to cache food for the long winter months.

The first hard frost of the season seems to send a strong message to beavers in northern climes. If they haven't already started, they begin to cut trees and branches and take them to a part of the pond near the lodge they will use for the winter. The first branches are carried to the bottom where the butt ends are shoved into the bottom mud. More branches are fixed this way and then branches are woven among the upright stems. As the pile becomes waterlogged and heavy, the branches sink. Still the beavers add more. Eventually, they have a large pile of sticks the size of an underwater lodge with some branches sticking above the water's surface.

The colony feeds on the emergent branches or clips them off and inserts them into the jackstrawed jumble below. Within a few weeks of completion, the first ice usually forms and from that point on, the colony depends almost exclusively on their food cache. The top branches freeze in the ice and are the source of food for the colony in late winter as the ice goes out.

Beavers in southern regions don't build food caches, but apparently the ability to do so is instinctive and just needs to be triggered by cold weather. Beavers which have been transplanted from south to north construct food caches in the fall and captive beavers raised from birth also demonstrate food caching behavior.

Food caches don't always have enough food to meet overwinter nutritional needs. Researchers have found, however, that while kits and yearlings usually gain weight in the winter, adults typically do not. This suggests that caches are primarily for kits and yearlings and that the adults can survive on fat reserves and limited food. Colonies comprised only of adults, however, usually store food. Perhaps when food is limited, adults give way to the needs of the younger animals.

During winter, beavers spend most of their time in the lodge sleeping, eating, and grooming. An occupied lodge will typically

have a layer of frost on the top where the warm breath of the animals meets the cool winter air. Beavers try to delay winter and hasten spring by working against the ice. The formation of the first ice on a pond spurs a beaver colony to break off the new ice around the food cache, in front of the dam, and near the lodge. They use their weight and either pull down the ice with their forepaws or stand on it until it breaks. Thicker ice is broken by forcefully butting it from below with the head and shoulders.

When food supplies are limited, beavers may emerge in mid or late winter to cut down trees. Otter holes kept open throughout the winter provide exits and a beaver may waddle across deep snow to fell an aspen and drag it back to the hole. Extremely cold weather keeps beavers below the ice, but days above fourteen degrees Fahrenheit seem acceptable for emergence.

85

When winter caches run out, beavers are forced to leave
the pond to cut down trees for food.

Beavers were perhaps the most hunted animal in North America
from the 1500s through the 1800s.

Survival Challenges

Through the eyes of a meat-eater, a beaver looks like an attractive potential meal, a solidly packed, but not too large, bundle of flesh with no obvious dangerous defensive features like antlers or sharp hooves. No doubt, many predators check the site of a beaver colony from time to time looking for an easy meal.

While a kit or yearling beaver might be fairly easy for a predator to catch, an adult male or female probably puts up quite a tussle and even drives off a predator occasionally. The large front incisors are formidable weapons, to which more than a few beaver trappers, dogs, and some predators can attest. Cornered beavers can put on a good show of aggression as well.

Predators

The beaver's semi-aquatic lifestyle renders it fairly invulnerable to predation while it is in the water. River otters and mink take their share of young beavers, but don't often try to catch an adult. Large northern pike or muskies in northern lakes may occasionally catch a beaver kit from a colony in a large lake or river. On the Rio Grande, a Mexican fisherman brought in a catfish weighing over forty pounds which had the remains of a small beaver in its stomach.

On land, beavers are vulnerable to wolves, bears, coyotes, lynx, bobcats, and wolverines. Of these, only wolves make beavers a regular part of their cuisine. Plunge holes, canals, and an uncanny ability to stay within escape distance of the water limit mortality from predation. However, during food shortages, when beavers are forced to forage farther and farther from the water, they suffer greater losses.

During the winter, when beavers are trapped under the ice and feeding from their underwater food caches, they are not vulnerable to most predators. Wolves have been seen on top of beaver lodges in winter sniffing at the ventilation hole and pawing at the roof. But the frozen mud and logs are far too sturdy to be broken in.

If a colony runs out of food in late winter or early spring, however, they are forced to cut through the ice and to search for food on land. At these times, their vulnerability is high. Beavers typically are most vulnerable to predation in the spring when they are hungrily seeking fresh food, and in the fall when they are cutting trees to make the winter food cache.

Wolves prey primarily on deer or moose and rely on smaller mammals like rabbits to a lesser degree. In many wolf packs across their range in Canada and the United States, beavers comprise up to twenty percent of the diet. On Isle Royale in the middle of Lake Superior, the wolves feed primarily on moose, but take beavers for around ten percent of their food. Beavers make up about a sixth of the diet for wolves in Minnesota and Wisconsin. In the Algonquin Park of Ontario, a long-term study of wolves indicated that beavers became an increasingly important part of wolves' diets as the density of white-tailed deer decreased. When deer hit their lowest level, beavers made up more than half of the food wolves ate.

When beavers are at a low density and there are plenty of other foods for them, wolves probably rarely actively hunt for beaver. They are more likely to chance upon them as they are making their rounds through their territories. On Isle Royale, where the percentage of beavers in wolves' diets has fluctuated

Beavers are almost invulnerable to predation in the water,
but are at risk on land.

over the years, researchers closely monitoring wolves have found that the number of lakes and streams influences the travelways of wolves. They have to skirt many lakes and ponds during the ice-free season and thus, come upon beavers almost as a matter of course.

On the Rio Grande, I only found the remains of one beaver that had been preyed upon. The partially covered pile of bones and hair suggested a member of the cat family. The large scats and paw marks nearby unequivocally identified the killer—a mountain lion.

Natural Causes

Beavers die primarily from diseases, starvation, and accidents. Sudden snow melts in the spring can flood lodges and trap beavers under the ice. Enormous floods on the Rio Grande happened every few years when violent thunderstorms in northern Mexico filled a reservoir on the Rio Conchos, and the Mexican officials opened the gates to save the dam. Without warning, the river would rise ten to twenty feet, sending uprooted trees, dead animals, and other debris downstream. Beavers were flooded out of their dens and sought refuge on the river banks.

The most common disease afflicting beavers and causing widespread death is tularemia. Tularemia, also known as rabbit fever and deerfly fever, is an infectious disease transmitted primarily by ticks and deerflies. Outbreaks of tularemia in beavers often leads to epidemics and deaths of many animals in a watershed. Sick beavers typically lose weight an become lethargic before death. Occasional tularemia outbreaks decimated beaver populations in Minnesota, Manitoba, and Ontario in the early 1950s.

I have had one close encounter with a sick beaver. One day, while I was counting small willow trees that had been felled by beaver along the Rio Grande, I heard what sounded like raspy breathing. I couldn't locate the sound at first, but eventually followed a feeding trail down to the river's edge where I found a

large beaver lying on the ground. I froze in my tracks and didn't move, hoping to not scare the beaver away. After standing stock still for a minute or two, I realized that the beaver had its eyes closed and appeared to be sleeping.

I took two or three slow and careful steps toward the beaver and it still laid there with its eyes closed. That brought me within a couple of feet of the animal. I figured it would open its eyes at any moment and be gone into the river. To get a better look, I slowly kneeled down hoping my knee joints wouldn't crack. At this point, the beaver was within reach. I crouched there for several minutes studying the animal. It had no apparent injuries, but seemed to have labored breathing. It had no idea I was there.

My knees were starting to ache from the uncomfortable squatting position and I knew I would soon have to move. As I considered standing up, I realized I had never touched a wild beaver. Would I ever have a better chance? After quick

Beavers often feed and groom themselves in shallow water where escape to deep water is easy.

consideration of what might go wrong if I did, I slowly reached out one hand to just above the beaver's back and held it there for a few seconds. Then, I slowly lowered it and placed it lightly on the back.

At first, the beaver didn't respond to my touch. Then, it opened its eyes and looked around. I stood up quickly and the beaver focused on me, its eyes full of what I had to believe was amazement. Slowly, but with decided purpose, it turned and slid into the water without even slapping its tail on the water. As I stood in the willow thicket, I had to convince myself that all of what I had just done had actually happened.

For days later, I wondered why this beaver was on the river bank in the middle of the day and why it had allowed me to approach and touch it. I concluded it must have been old or sick. Two weeks later, when I next visited the colony, I found a beaver's skeleton in nearly the same place. Although I couldn't

prove that the skeleton was from the beaver I had touched, I could only surmise that it was. I also felt sure that it had died from some malady and that its flesh had been scavenged.

The   Human   Element

Over the last three hundred years, North American beavers have been trapped by humans to varying degrees of intensity. Humans have unquestionably been the largest source of predation during that period. Because of significant trapping pressure throughout their range, it wasn't until Ph. D. student Harry Hodgdon studied an unexploited beaver population in Massachusetts, that we had an idea of what "non-human" beaver mortality might be.

Beavers returned to Massachusetts in 1928 after an absence of

Beavers detect predators primarily by smell and sound.

nearly two hundred years. One of the places they moved into was Quabbin Reservoir and its associated streams and rivers in the western part of the state. Working with a marked population, Hodgdon found very little mortality, as low as only one or two percent per year. Admittedly, the area didn't support wolves and other large predators. However, bobcats were present and there was at least one incident of a bobcat killing a yearling beaver. Nonetheless, in the absence of trapping and large populations of predators, beavers appear to have high survival rates.

The oldest recorded beaver in the wild was twenty years old. In captivity, they may live to thirty or more years. Living to a ripe old age may not be so common in areas of inadequate habitat and where populations are dense. There, food shortages cause more frequent colony movement and long movements by dispersing juveniles. Many more of those beavers likely die from starvation and the pressures of predation.

Although rarely mentioned in the scientific literature, one other source of mortality seems to be pretty common to me—road kill. Now, perhaps this is because I drive thousands of miles every year and because I live in an area of dense beaver populations. However, I am amazed by the number of beavers I see lying on the sides of roads, victims of automobile accidents. I have even come across live beavers working their way down road ditches or shoulders and once tried to chase a beaver to the safety of the woods in northern Minnesota. This beaver would have none of it and stayed on the shoulder, occasionally turning and hissing at me for hurrying it along at a pace faster than it had set for itself.

While today's demand for animal fur by the fashion industry is low enough to discourage most beaver trappers, beavers continue to be trapped for the purpose of removing them from areas in which they are a nuisance. Every year, private landowners, townships, and resource conservation agencies hire hundreds of trappers and pays thousands of dollars to get beavers out of trout streams, orchards, lakes, waterfowl impoundments, and roadside wetlands where their dams and insatiable appetites get in the way of human objectives for dry roads, working culverts, trees, and high quality trout fisheries.

Tree-cutting and flooding caused by beavers are often
in conflict with human desires.

Young beavers learn which kinds of food to eat
by watching their parents and older siblings.

The
Reproductive
Cycle

Beavers are driven by the same forces that govern all life, particularly the need to pass on copies of their genes to future generations of beavers, and more specifically, to pass on more copies than their neighbors. Year after year, beavers repeat the same cycle of events which start with pregnancy and end with the establishment of a new family group by their offspring.

It all begins in the winter with breeding. As with most wild animals, copulation is rarely observed by people. Early scientists mistook upright wrestling behavior for breeding. Later observations revealed that copulation occurs in the water or in bank dens or the lodge.

Breeding

Adult female beavers come into estrus between November and March depending on what part of North America they live in. Northern beavers breed between January and March while those in southern latitudes breed as early as November and December. The estrus period is short, just ten to twelve hours, and is followed by another estrus two weeks later if the adult

97

Next pages: Male and female beavers swim together
during the breeding season.

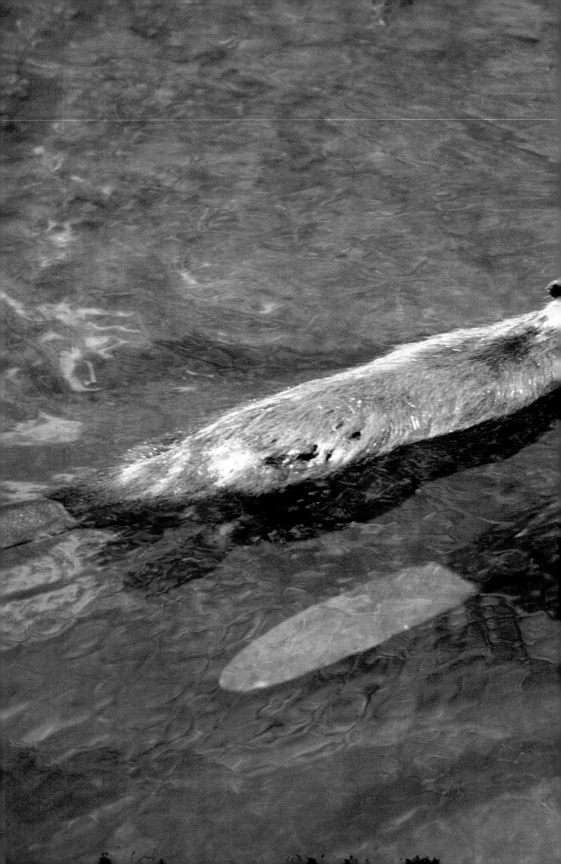

female is not fertilized the first time.

Female beavers become sexually mature either at one-and-a-half years old or at two-and-a-half years. In the mid-portion of their geographic range and when food conditions are favorable, they can become pregnant at the younger age. In northern and southern latitudes, however, first breeding doesn't usually happen until their third winter.

Typically, only one female in a colony breeds. On rare occasions, researchers have found two breeding females in one colony. Pregnant females carry their fetuses for one hundred to one hundred ten days. Poor nutrition of adults going into winter sometimes leads to losses of young before birth.

For many years, scientists believed that during the breeding

100

Male beavers sense the breeding readiness
of females in part by smell.

season the normally sociable colony went through profound changes. They thought that the two-year-olds, which have been living with their one-year-old siblings and parents, were either forcibly driven out of the colony or left of their own volition. Additionally, it was widely believed that the adult male and other members of the colony were banished from the main lodge where the kits would be born. However, an intensive study of beaver colonies with individually marked beavers conducted by Harry Hodgdon in the late 1970s, and detailed observations by Hope Ryden and other naturalists, revealed a far more complex set of circumstances.

Kits

As birthing time approaches, the adult female spends more and more time in the lodge. The expectant mother and other members of the colony make a soft bedding by cutting small sticks and bringing them into the lodge where the fibers are pulled apart. Grass (if available) is occasionally brought in from outside and used for either bedding or food. The walls are plastered with mud and protruding sticks are gnawed, presumably to create a safe environment for the newborns.

Beaver kits are born between February and June, again depending on latitude. The typical litter has three or four young with a range of one to nine being possible. It takes anywhere from two-and-a-half to three days for the female to give birth. During birthing, the female sits upright with her tail underneath her and pointing forward. Canadian researcher Francoise Patenaude observed beavers being born in the wild by constructing a viewing station in part of a beaver lodge. She saw the adult male and one of the yearlings gather around the female as she delivered the kits. The female licked the kits soon after birth and ate the placenta, as is common in many mammals.

Baby beavers are a little over a foot long including the tail when born and weigh around a pound. They are fully furred, their eyes are partially open, and their incisor teeth are already

101

in place. Beaver kits have fur color varying from reddish to brown to black.

The kits start to nurse within an hour of birth. Female beavers have four nipples and so may not be able to nurse all of their young at once. Kits nurse frequently and irregularly throughout the day, oftentimes engaging in nine or more separate nursing periods lasting between five and thirty minutes. While suckling, the kits press their mother's nipples rhythmically with their forepaws, and like human babies, often fall asleep as they nurse.

One morning, as I watched a colony of beavers in Big Bend National Park, I saw the adult female in the colony swim to shore where she was joined by two small beaver kits whose age I guessed at a month or so. I had never seen the kits before and almost forgot to take notes. They mewed and whined until their mother turned on her side and exposed her nipples for them. They eagerly began to suckle as I watched in amazement from only thirty or so feet away. The kits made sounds of sucking while their mother moaned softly.

The feeding period lasted somewhere between five and ten minutes—I forgot to time it—and I felt incredibly fortunate to be able to watch. Never again during my year of research on the Rio Grande did I see a mother with young.

Not all of the kits nurse at the same time and they don't seem to show a preference for which nipple they choose unless there are only one or two kits in the litter. Then, they choose the lower nipples which produce twice as much milk as the upper ones.

Mother beavers produce milk for two to three months. However, beaver kits start to supplement their diets with solid food starting as early as a few weeks after birth, but more consistently at around a month old. They are fully weaned by six to eight weeks. Their first food is often a leafy branch brought into the lodge by the male or the yearlings.

Beaver kits eat the foods their parents bring to them at first and then start to forage on their own. They seem to mimic the adults, nibbling at whatever their father or mother is eating. A mother beaver sometimes hold food in her mouth for the kits and

Food is brought into the lodge before kits
venture out into the pond.

often eats foods she wants the kits to try. That doesn't sound so different from human mothers trying to convince their toddlers to eat their vegetables by showing them how to do it first.

Kits stay in the lodge until they are two months old although they have been in the water in the escape holes in the lodge. They are tended in the lodge by a baby sitter, usually their mother or one of the yearlings. These older siblings keep them from falling into the escape holes while they are very young. Kits, being extremely buoyant, can't navigate the underwater passages until they are older.

Kits grow quickly on their diet of nutritious milk and soft green vegetation. By the end of their first month, they weigh four pounds. At four months as summer comes to a close, they have attained ten pounds. At six months old they weigh around twelve pounds and by the time their parents are breeding again, they are

nearly twenty pounds. When they complete their first year, they have attained nearly half their adult weight—twenty-five pounds.

Young female beavers tend to produce smaller litters in their first few years than their older counterparts. Normally, about an equal number of male and female kits are born, although there tends to be slightly more males. No one seems to know what the chances are of a female bearing all females or all males or just how much variation there is in sex ratios among different litters.

Like many large mammals and birds, but unlike most rodents, beavers have evolved into creatures that invest a large amount of energy into bearing and raising their young. It takes a beaver years to reach sexual maturity and to acquire survival skills necessary to start its own family. The long period of development for the young suggests that they must learn many of the skills they will need in life, and that not all beaver behavior is instinctive.

105

Kits follow their parents on some inland foraging trips.

Kits are groomed and nursed frequently
by their mother.

C h a p t e r   8

Social Behavior

Beavers are highly social mammals, living in family groups, cooperating in gathering and storing food, and building elaborate structures. As such, they have evolved a system of communicating a variety of messages that help the group get along.

Basic Communication

While beavers may use subtle body postures to communicate, they don't have the obvious signals used by animals such as wolves. Instead, they rely primarily on sound and scent.

Beavers do not have a wide repertoire of vocalizations. The sounds they make can best be described as whines, whimpers, whistles, hisses, and growls. Growls and hisses are heard only infrequently and in the context of aggression. People who have live-trapped problem beavers hear beavers hiss as they approach the cage. Close observers of beavers in the wild hear growls and hisses most when adults refuse food to begging yearlings.

The whine is far and away the most common beaver vocalization. Kits start whining for food and attention soon after they are born. The whines can actually be heard from outside the lodge and I have heard kits whining inside bank dens. Kits continue to whine when they are in their first summer. Whining often occurs as they swim close to an adult or older beaver. It is typically associated with food begging behavior. Unlike the yearlings, however, kits are rarely refused food by their parents who give away the choice morsels of tender bark and leaves.

The adult female is the focus of most whining. She endures the advances of not just her young of the year, but the yearlings as well when they want food or attention. Whining is also associated with other social situations like play and grooming.

A   Warning   To   All

The best known sound beavers make is the tail slap. The sometimes thunderous slap of the tail on the water has long been understood to serve as an alarm for other beavers and perhaps a distraction to potential predators. It is usually associated with a warning dive in which the body is submerged in a violent splash.

Beavers slap their tails when they see, hear, or smell a predator nearby. They slap their tail on the water, dive, and resurface quickly to determine where the intruder has gone. If the danger is still close by, they often slap the water again perhaps trying to encourage the source of disturbance to unveil itself.

Most of us have heard tail slaps, but in all of my years of watching beavers, I have only seen a beaver slap its tail a few times and then just from the corner of my eye. Thank goodness for people like Harry Hodgdon who watched beavers slap their tails hundreds of times at him and other disturbances to their otherwise peaceful home on the Quabbin Reservoir.

Tail slapping almost always occurs in the water although a captive beaver will slap its tail in a cage and beavers on land running toward the water sometimes make thuds with their tails as they hurry along.

Tail slaps are almost never the result of a beaver being suddenly disturbed or startled. Instead, it seems to be the culmination of stimuli eventually pushing the beaver over a psychological

threshold of discomfort. Smell seems to be the strongest cue. Beavers have poor sight and keen hearing, but it is the nose that makes final confirmation of danger. When faced with scent or sound, scent appears to be eleven times stronger in eliciting a tail slap. Sight alone rarely results in a tail slap, but usually causes a beaver to investigate further.

Different odors elicit variable responses. The smell of humans, wolves, bobcats, and dogs usually cause tail slaps. The smell of a deer or moose or other non-threatening animal is paid little heed although yearling and kit beavers sometimes slap when deer or moose are present, probably in a playful fashion.

A beaver disturbed enough to tail slap quickly raises its head and tail above the water with its back arched. The outstretched

109

A beaver about to perform a tail slap raises
it vertically above the water.

After a tail slap the entire body is submerged and
water cascades in all directions.

tail is raised directly overhead. Almost in unison, the head and tail are snapped downward at the water and the hind feet, which start underwater, are kicked backward breaking the water's surface and throwing water into the air just after the tail strikes. The head is still above water when the tail slaps, but is underwater just a fraction of a second later starting a shallow dive which lasts around two seconds.

When the beaver surfaces, it assumes an alert posture with its head held high out of the water. Typically, it orients itself toward the source of the disturbance and tests the air for the giveaway smell. If the disturbance is detected again, there may be more tail slaps. If the disturbance has been minor, the beaver may slap only once and resume the alert posture while it patrols the area.

Other beavers in the colony react to the tail slap of a family member. If they are already in deep water and thus, relatively safe, they pay little attention and stay in the water. Those beavers in shallow water or along the shoreline usually move to deeper water where their safety increases. Beavers feeding in the adjacent forest react predictably by hurrying into the water. Researchers have determined that the adult female in the colony initiates a tail slap more often than other colony members, but that adult males slap most for any one disturbance. Other beavers in the colony move to deep water more readily when the female does a tail slap compared to when they hear tail slaps from the male, yearlings, or kits. Kits engage in tail slapping infrequently. Although they have been observed tail slapping in captivity at twenty-eight days and in the wild at fifty-seven, they typically don't start tail slapping with any frequency until after the ice-out of their first year.

Many of us have a vivid memory or two of being surprised by a beaver slapping its tail on the water in response to our presence. My field study of beavers on the Rio Grande gave me many such memories. I often watched a colony in the early morning darkness and gradual coming of dawn. Although the beavers usually ignored my presence for a while, they eventually became nervous and slapped their tails. This almost always signaled the end of my observation period. Occasionally, a beaver would swim close to where I stood waist-deep in the stream and slap its tail from just a few feet away, soaking me with the spray.

Another colony I tried to observe during the early morning hours lived several miles downstream from the closest access to the river. I typically drove for an hour to the landing, carried my canoe on my shoulders in the dark down a path I had committed to memory, waited for just enough light to see, and paddled downstream to the colony site where I could watch and count the beavers for a short time.

One morning, I left much too early and arrived at the landing more than an hour before there would be enough light to see. Knowing that I would fall asleep in my car and miss the observation period if I tried to wait, I carried my canoe to the river and floated downstream. It was so dark that I kept bumping into the riverbank and banging into logs, so I pulled over to the side of the river to wait for the necessary light. Lack of sleep overtook me right there in the canoe and I laid down in the bottom. Not many minutes must have past when I was wakened by the crash of a falling tree which sounded like it was going to land on me. Not remembering where I was, I sat up quickly only to bump my head hard against the cross piece between the gunwales of the canoe. The racket I created made a beaver slap its tail right next to the canoe and the beaver felling the tree on shore rushed to the water where it dove, resurfaced, and slapped its tail. The rest of the colony members rushed to the water and returned to their bank dens. At that moment, startled, with a throbbing head, and a ruined observation period, I seriously questioned my choice in studying beavers.

Scent Mounds

Vocalizations and tail slaps may not be nearly as important nor send as many specific messages as the odors beavers leave in strategic places throughout the colony. Beavers have a highly developed sense of smell and use it to discern among an intricate mixture of aromas which communicate important facts about what is happening in the colony.

112

Have you ever smelled a beaver? You may have done so without even knowing it if you like to canoe along the shoreline of lakes or down small streams. Despite living in central Maine where beavers are common, it took me until I was twenty-three years old before I figured out that the strangely sweet, musky smell I sometimes whiffed on my many canoe trips was made by a beaver.

Now, after years of using my nose to sniff out areas along the Rio Grande where beavers were active, I can't ignore the smell that always reminds me of a freshly curried horse. Follow your nose the next time you come across that aroma and you'll likely find yourself next to a small pile of scratched earth at the water's edge. Look closely and you'll notice that the earth is discolored.

Beavers have a strongly developed sense of smell.

114

Beavers manipulate small twigs like a person
eating corn on the cob.

Lean down close to the pile and breathe in deeply. Cement that smell in your brain—beavers.

The source of what I find to be a most enjoyable bouquet is a pair of glands located near the base of the beaver's tail. Beavers have two sets of glands which lie beneath the skin between their pelvic girdle and anal opening which is called a cloaca. One set, the castor glands, produces a waxy substance called castoreum which is mixed with urine in the cloaca and sprayed on an area of scratched earth or a small pile of mud and vegetation.

Beavers collect mud, twigs, and vegetation from the bottom of lakes and rivers and carry the load to the water's edge where they set it down. The forepaws are used to collect and carry the materials which are held tightly under the chin as the animal swims. Upon reaching shore or shallow water, a beaver assumes a rather awkward walking style using only the two hind feet for locomotion and the tail as a counterbalance. They place the materials on the ground and spread it around with their forepaws.

After putting the material on the ground, the beaver moves over the mound until its cloaca is over the site. Then, it hunches its back, partially everts its cloaca causing protrusion of the openings of the anal glands, and makes a rapid series of kicking motions with one of its hind legs as the castoreum is deposited. Sometimes, a beaver will rub its abdomen with its forepaws just before making the deposit.

As soon as the castoreum has been sprayed, the beaver starts to walk away stiff-legged with the protruding anal glands still over the marked area. The tail is held rigid and out straight so it doesn't drag over the mound. As soon as it has cleared the mound, the beaver normally rushes quickly to the water.

Adult males initiate marking and add more material to scent mounds than any other members of the colony. The adult female is next in frequency. Kits rarely mark before they are a year old.

Individuals don't have their own scent mounds. Observers have seen most members of a colony marking the same scent mound one right after another, some depositing new materials before spraying and some coming empty-handed. An adult could spray the same mound up to a dozen times in one evening during the peak scent marking season.

Scent mounds come in a variety of shapes and sizes. Almost all of the "mounds" I found along the Rio Grande looked like the beaver had quickly made a few scratches with its front paws, straddled it, and sprayed. One day, however, on a long river trip, I came across a mound that was six inches high and a couple of feet long. The aroma from that mound could be smelled all the way across the river. I had to look around at the tracks left by the builders to calm my fear that one last giant beaver had survived into the modern world! Beavers in other parts of the country sometimes make large scent mounds, depositing new material on old mounds and marking the tops and sides of them. Beavers in Montana hold the unofficial record for the largest scent mounds documented by researchers, making some that are over two feet high.

Scent marking by mammals is typically associated with territorial behavior. Early naturalists assumed this to be the case for

116

Beavers are territorial and defend the colony
area from intruders.

beaver, but the placement and use of scent mounds don't support solely a territorial function. A husband-and-wife team of scientists, Ronald and Linda Butler, studying beavers in Acadia National Park on the coast of Maine in the late 1970s discovered that scent mounds are normally constructed in parts of the colony where beavers are most active. In addition, colonies with a higher probability of being visited by beavers from other colonies or transient beavers passing through build many more scent mounds.

Most scent mounds I found on the Rio Grande were constructed at the ends of trails leading to feeding areas in the floodplain forest. The beaver colonies on my study area often had distinct boundaries on the upstream and downstream ends because there would be a stretch of river without a floodplain forest. If the scent mounds had served a territorial function, I would have expected them to be placed near the territory boundaries. Similarly, the study in Maine found five of six scent mounds constructed in the vicinity of feeding trails, feeding areas where beavers brought their food, and places on the bank where beavers regularly groomed themselves.

On my canoe trips through Wisconsin, Minnesota, and Ontario, I have stopped to look at many scent mounds which I usually discovered with my nose. In almost every case, they were associated with obvious trails back to areas where beavers had recently cut down trees or a place on the bank worn free of vegetation from frequent use.

I counted over two hundred scent mounds in the five colonies I visited every couple of weeks for a year in Texas. It appeared that a new mound was constructed in most cases. Rarely did I find a mound that looked large enough to be new scratching at an old site. The number of mounds constructed may have been influenced by beavers from other colonies moving up and down the river. Two colonies which were over a mile from the nearest colony had very few mounds constructed during the year, while the other three colonies which had neighbors right at their boundaries had over fifty mounds each.

In Maine, the Butlers found that the beavers deposited new mud, leaves, twigs, and castoreum on the same mounds during the summer. Over the course of the season, some mounds got quite large. The colonies making the most mounds were those with other beaver families nearby.

In areas where water levels are stable, scent mounds are used over and over. On the Rio Grande and other rivers where water level fluctuates almost daily, scent marking is done with small mounds used just once or a few times.

If scent marking in beavers doesn't send a territorial message, what does it mean? The researchers in Maine thought that scent marking transmitted information about the physiological status of individual colony members, such as females in estrus, sexually immature yearlings, and the dominant male. Experiments have demonstrated that beavers can discriminate sexual differences based on deposits of castoreum. It seems that there is a variety of information stored in that alluring scent.

Scent marking is limited to periods of open water for beavers living in the North. The peak of activity varies, but seems to be typically soon after the ice goes out. Around Maine and Massachusetts, it starts around mid-March or early April and ends in mid-June with another low level of activity in October and November. In the southern portions of beaver range, scent mounds are constructed year-round. On my study area in the Southwest, beavers didn't show any discernible pattern of seasonal marking.

In areas where ice forms for an extended period, ice-out represents the time when the colony has access to its entire territory for the first time in several months. There is usually intense scent marking for about two weeks all over the colony site. Then, the frequency decreases and becomes concentrated at the lodge, feeding sites, and other activity areas. Late spring snowfalls bring a rapid end to scent marking as beavers do not make scent mounds on snow.

Beavers have the ability to mark at any time of the year. Juveniles dispersing to a new home site normally mark for a few weeks after they set up in new quarters. Similarly, a family that moves its colony site any time between ice-out and freeze-up marks as it is getting settled into new surroundings. A lone adult having lost its mate often marks intensively for a while, perhaps

advertising to passers through that there is a vacancy for the appropriate sex. Not surprisingly, dispersing beavers rarely, if ever, mark as they are passing through occupied territories.

Getting Along

Unlike the proverbial "rats in a cage" which are unable to stand the stress of living in close quarters, beavers spend a lot of time living shoulder to shoulder, and do so without much aggression. When you think about spending the winter in the tight confines of a beaver lodge, it is remarkable that beavers not only avoid serious fights, but they actually seem to enjoy the company of their family members. Over the eons, they have evolved behaviorally and developed a social system which results in apparent harmony within the colony.

119

Beavers occasionally work together on tasks.

Next pages: Dam maintenance and repair are a team effort.

As with many social groups of animals, young are the center of attention and the focus of most colony activity. Beavers give almost constant care to their kits and each member of the colony participates. When the kits are first brought out of the lodge in the late spring or early summer, it isn't unusual to see them swimming right next to their mother or an older sibling. Young kits, like loon chicks and young grebes, are often allowed to piggyback rides from their parents and siblings. They ride on the back or tail and sometimes hold onto shoulder fur or an ear with their forepaws or teeth.

Kits are provided with ample food in the lodge, and even after they are swimming on their own. Older beavers often allow kits to usurp the food item they have been feeding with little

more than a half-hearted attempt to rebuff the begging, and rarely do they move away. Because the kits have much to learn from their family, it is important for the adults to allow the kits to watch and imitate their behavior while they are feeding or cutting down trees.

Kits often engage in play. As they swim together or with another colony member, they dive under or porpoise over the other beavers. The adults and older siblings don't completely lose this playfulness with age. Observers regularly report beavers swimming in tandem, diving in synchrony, and playing tug of war with sticks.

Play may serve to help bind the colony together, but there are moments of stress and aggression which threaten the stability

123

Kits beg for food from their parents and older siblings.

of the society. Squabbles over food and space are not uncommon and need to be resolved without resorting to fighting, which could result in injury. The dependence on each colony member to play a role in all aspects of colony life seems to be a strong inhibitor to serious fighting.

The most common form of dispute resolution for beavers is a shoving or wrestling match, which usually occurs in shallow water. Beavers either stand upright and push against each other with their forepaws or go shoulder to shoulder in a test of strength. The loser is pushed into deeper water, but there is no groveling or submissive posturing as seen in wolves and other species. Instead, when the fight is over, the animals go about their routine business.

Rarely does an aggressive encounter escalate to a fight in which biting is used, suggesting that beavers have strong inhibitors against the use of their teeth as weapons. In four years of close observations of a beaver colony in New York, Hope Ryden observed biting only a few times and these were just quick nips to the hindquarters which drew no blood. On the other hand, other researchers have observed more violent fights between a beaver on its home turf and an intruder that won't leave. Starting as a typical wrestling match, these encounters escalate in intensity and serious bites are inflicted. It is easy to imagine that a bite could cause death considering the force of the jaws that can cut through a small sapling in one bite.

Beavers are fastidious animals and spend hours every day grooming their fur. Grooming periods are another time in which social bonds are made. The adults of the colony and other like-aged beavers often pair off during a grooming session. They start by grooming their own coats with their forepaws and grooming claws on the hind feet. After a while, they reach down and squeeze some castoreum from their cloacas and rub it on their chests. This incites the other beaver to begin some mutual grooming, which is done by gently mouthing the fur around the head, neck, and shoulders. Curiously, mutual grooming does not involve the use of the forepaws of the other beaver.

Beavers seem to enjoy the mutual contact during grooming, but it is not limited just to that activity. Intensive observations

suggest that beavers regularly seek out other colony members and engage in everything from quick nuzzling of faces while swimming to more intimate sessions of nuzzling, sometimes called "kissing," on shore. Mated pairs sometimes crawl on shore and sit for minutes on end making soft vocalizations and rubbing their heads and faces together.

The suite of vocalizations, tail-slapping, scent mound construction, and physical interactions creates an intricate system of communication for beavers, a system whose importance is driven by the need for the colony to spend its time and energy on cooperative behavior.

125

Beavers are fastidious groomers so that their fur stays clean and waterproofed.

Beavers may move many miles to find a new colony site.

M o v e m e n t s

Beavers expend a great deal of energy and time constructing elaborate waterworks, but the stability they desire is only short-lived—for beavers dance to the rhythm of a tune of constant, if subtle, change. Most beaver colonies are transitory in time and space; few persist in the same place over the course of a decade and most for just a few years.

An established colony makes short moves over the course of a year and among years. Harry Hodgdon found that all beaver families shifted their activity center at least once over six years and most families shifted annually. An activity center shift involves construction of a new lodge or movement into an old lodge after it has been refurbished. These movements occur primarily in the fall as the colony prepares itself for winter.

Beaver families also make short distance moves to new home sites outside of their normal range of activities. This may be a move up or down the watershed they are inhabiting. Hodgdon found adult females initiating these moves primarily in the summer after birth of the kits. At the new site, the entire family puts its efforts into construction of new dams, lodges, canals, and channels. The kits may be left behind with an older sibling at first and then escorted to the new home site by one of the adults. Hope Ryden described such a move by the colony she studied intensively for four years. After getting the new colony site in order, the adult male returned to the old colony area and brought the kits to their new home.

Occasionally, beaver families make long distance moves, but these journeys are usually reserved for young adult members of the family who strike off on their own. Adults and two-year-olds sometimes leave the colony abruptly in the summer and are gone for a few days to a week. Adult males and non-breeding adult females may be exploring for potential new colony sites.

There was a long-held belief that two-year-old beavers were forced out of their families around the time of birth of new kits. Intensive observations by a handful of researchers has shown this to be a far too rigid interpretation of what actually occurs.

In many families the two-year-olds do leave never to return,

127

but some do return after being gone for a while and are accepted back into the colony. Their original departure is never associated with aggression from their parents and seems to be of their own volition. Some colonies, contrary to popular belief, are comprised of adults, kits of the year, and siblings from two or three other years. Food supply and the individual instincts of each beaver may be the strongest factors determining when juveniles strike off on their own.

Dispersal by juveniles and young adults typically are long distance movements as opposed to a simple movement up or down the watershed or to a different part of a lake, although there are exceptions. Overland movement is common and some beavers cross major highways and harsh terrain to find a new watershed. A dispersing beaver moves slowly, up to a mile per night. They usually restrict their movements to evening hours and hole up in abandoned lodges, under tree roots on banks, and in culverts during the day.

When a disperser comes to an area occupied by a beaver family, it may pause up to an hour at the edge of the colony smelling the air and investigating any scent mounds present. Once it decides to proceed through the area, the beaver moves quickly and takes a direct route. It does not feed, stop to make scent mounds, or attempt to seek out the resident beavers. The residents show no interest in dispersers even when they pass at a close distance. A disperser may become part of an existing colony if its inspection of scent mounds reveals a bachelor or widowed female.

Some movements of dispersing beavers are legendary in their length. Harry Hodgdon discovered one of his study animals two hundred and fifty miles from its natal colony. The natural movement of one ear-tagged beaver in Alaska was over two hundred miles. Some marked beavers have shown up on the opposite side of mountain ranges from their home colony and others have crossed miles of agricultural lands to get to their new homes.

Even a beaver on the move has to stop to eat.

130

Unlike most other mammals, beavers continue
to grow throughout their lives.

A Restoration Success Story

Beavers occur in North America, Europe, and north-central Asia. There is no record of the pre-human extent of beaver range in Eurasia, but they likely occurred wherever there was water and suitable food to last them through the winter. The southern limit of their historical Eurasian range is unknown.

Historical Numbers and Range

In North America, prior to settlement by Europeans, beavers inhabited virtually the entire continent. Their northernmost limit was probably the mouth of the MacKenzie River in Canada's Northwest Territories. They likely occurred throughout Alaska, except for the Arctic slope from Point Hope east to the Canadian border. Their northern limit in Canada was the treeless tundra northwest and northeast of Hudson Bay. In the United States, they occurred from coast to coast with absences only in parts of the arid Southwest and Great Plains and in southern Florida.

Their original range in Mexico is unknown, but Aldo Leopold's son, Starker, who studied the fauna of Mexico in the

131

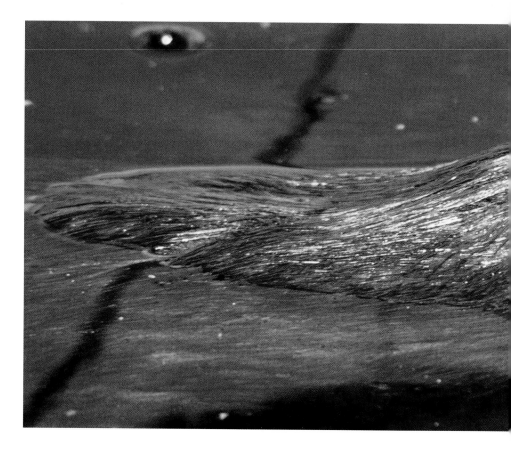

mid-1900s, found them on the Colorado River and the Rio Grande and their tributaries in northern Mexico, as well as in some coastal streams of the western Gulf of Mexico.

No one will ever know the number of beavers in North America before the advent of the great trapping era. The naturalist Ernest Thompson Seton estimated the historical number of beavers at sixty million, which could have easily been low by fifty percent. To the settlers and explorers of the continent, their numbers must have seemed legion and virtually endless. They could hardly imagine that a century of intensive trapping would nearly wipe them out.

The Great Fur Rush

More than any other natural resource, the beaver was responsible for the opening of North America. In the absence of
beavers, it is unlikely that North America would have been
explored and settled as fast as it was.

Native peoples had been killing beavers and using their pelts
and meat long before Europeans arrived. As beavers were common all over, there probably wasn't trade in pelts at that time.

All that changed when early settlers arrived. They traded
with native people for beaver pelts. Eventually, they went into
the interior of the continent to acquire pelts of beaver and other
numerous furbearers for themselves.

Beavers numbered in the tens of millions before
the settlement of North America.

Next pages: The beaver's luxurious fur was coveted
by trappers and early settlers.

The French were particularly well known for their trappers. English, French, and Dutch fur companies, eager to feed the hunger of the European fur market, established posts and trading centers. The legendary voyageurs canoed and hiked throughout the wilds of what is now Canada and northern North America to trap beavers and bring their pelts to shipping centers such as St. Louis, Montreal, and Albany.

The fur trade led to the development of the rendezvous, an annual event at which trappers and voyageurs gathered at strategic locations to exchange pelts bound for shipping ports with supplies to get them through the next year. The rendezvous allowed trappers to stay in the interior and the fur companies enjoyed the benefit of reasonably rapid transport to their primary shipping centers.

It was the beaver that spawned the establishment of famous fur companies such as the Hudson Bay Company, the Northwest Company, and the Rocky Mountain Fur Company. Fortunes were made for the entrepreneurs who recognized the incredible resource of fur.

The life of the voyageur and his western counterpart, the mountain man, have been told across campfires for over a hundred years and are well chronicled. The songs of the French voyageurs live on today and hardy souls reenact the events of the rendezvous in places like Thunder Bay, Ontario, Prairie du Chien, Wisconsin, and Deer River, Minnesota annually.

It should be no surprise that the beaver pelt was the most common form of currency in the New World for a time. In fact, the value on trade goods was established in relationship to a beaver pelt. The best known of these examples is the famous Hudson's Bay wool blanket, a staple item for most trappers. Each blanket was given a "point" value recorded as a set of small lines woven into the blanket. A blanket with four lines was a "four-point" blanket which required four large beaver pelts for exchange. Smaller and thinner blankets with fewer points traded for fewer beaver pelts.

The romantic notion of the lives of voyageurs and mountain men would have been lost on the men who actually did that work. They suffered great hardship and danger, toiled long

Unregulated trapping nearly spelled the doom of beavers.

hours under less than ideal conditions, and paid the price for their choice of work. They were opportunists, making their living on the abundance of the beaver. They were exploiters who nearly trapped the beaver into extinction and who forever altered the lives of many native peoples. Their activities allowed the uncharted territory to be mapped and the continent to be settled quickly.

Changes in hat manufacturing caused a great crash in beaver pelt prices in the mid-1800s and the beaver populations were given relief from the virtual slaughter which was no less dramatic than that of the buffalo, but not nearly as well recorded nor played up by the media at that time.

138

The beaver's industriousness has been used
to restore degraded river systems.

Bringing Back the Beaver

The beaver nearly went the way of the passenger pigeon, the plains grizzly, the Carolina parakeet, and the great auk in North America. Instead, like the buffalo, enough remained after the great fur rush to repopulate some areas naturally. Unfortunately, beavers were literally trapped out of many watersheds with little hope that immigrants would find their way to these vacant habitats on their own.

In Europe, the situation was no better. By 1860, only a few populations were left in Europe on the Elbe River, along the lower stretches of the Rhone River in France, and in remote regions of southern Norway. In Asia, beavers were virtually extinct even across the broad expanse of Siberia.

Reintroduction efforts by humans brought the beaver back to many parts of their original range and the beavers did the rest themselves. In Europe, the Swedes got the ball rolling by importing some beavers from southern Norway. These spread throughout the country and into Finland. Today, almost all suitable habitats in Scandinavia now have beavers. Poland followed suit and the beaver is on the rebound there. In the 1970s West Germany imported beavers and released them in Bavaria along the Inn River and the Danube. In just fifteen years, the population had grown to over two hundred animals.

In North America, beaver restoration started with the closing of trapping seasons in the late 1800s. State wildlife agencies began transplanting beaver in the first decade of the 1900s. A few states, such as Minnesota, Wisconsin, and Michigan, were fortunate enough to have some remaining populations from which beavers were live-trapped and shipped all over the country, particularly to eastern states. Today, the restoration of beavers to states like Idaho, Wyoming, Utah, and Nevada continues; and along with the animals themselves comes the ecosystems for which they have become so famous.

Many western streams have become deep gullies which dry up in mid-summer due to overgrazing and other detrimental land uses. The Natural Resources Conservation Service (formerly the Soil Conservation Service) and other agencies are working with

139

ranchers to restore the composition, structure, and function of riparian areas by reintroducing beavers.

Beavers were so fertile and so mobile that they repopulated many areas within ten or twenty years. Without trapping and predation by large carnivores, which were also largely absent, their populations exploded in some areas and they started to cause damage to valuable timber lands, agricultural fields, roads, and irrigation ditches. The demand for fur was high at the same time and pressure was exerted on game departments to open a trapping season. At first, state wildlife agencies dealt with nuisance beavers by using their own trappers, who live-trapped many beavers and moved them to places where no beavers lived. Eventually, they determined that limited trapping seasons were biologically sound and beaver trapping became legal again.

From the 1930s on, beavers continued to move into areas they once inhabited. The vagaries of the fur market affected their populations locally, but the overall trend was one of increase. Today, with the demand for fur at a low and the value of beaver pelts barely worth the effort for a trapper, beavers have pushed into even marginal areas, including road ditches, farm ponds, commercial wild rice paddies, and cranberry bogs.

It is safe to say that beavers have been restored to most, if not all, of their original range in North America even though much of the range looks a lot different than it did two hundred years ago. It is estimated that beavers number in the millions again. They are present throughout the continent. The beaver is back!

The beaver has been restored to nearly all of its
historic range in North America.

Beaver populations are secure in most areas where waters run.

Further Reading

Hilfiker, Earl L. *Beavers: Water, Wildlife, and History*. Interlaken, NY: Windswept Press, 1990.

Hodgdon, Harry E. "Social Dynamics and Behavior Within an Unexploited Beaver (*Castor canadensis*) Population." Ph.D. thesis, University of Massachusetts, Amherst, 1978.

Richards, Dorothy. *Beaversprite: My Years Building an Animal Sanctuary*. San Francisco: Chronicle Books, 1977.

Rue, Leonard Lee III. *The World of the Beaver*. New York: Lippincott, 1964.

————. *Meet the Beaver*. New York: Dodd, Mead, Co., 1986.

Ryden, Hope. *Lily Pond: Four Years with a Family of Beavers*. New York: Morrow, 1989.

Shelton, Philip. "Ecological Studies of Beavers, Wolves, and Moose in Isle Royale National Park, Michigan." Ph.D. thesis, Purdue University, 1966.

Strong, Paul I. V. "Beaver-Cottonwood Interactions and Beaver Ecology in Big Bend National Park, Texas." Master's thesis, Oklahoma State University, Stillwater, 1981.